YESTERDAY, TODAY AND FOREVER

A Palestinian Pilgrimage

YESTERDAY, TODAY AND FOREVER

A Palestinian Pilgrimage

By

Siham Musallam Brown

JOHN RITCHIE LTD
CHRISTIAN PUBLICATIONS

40 Beansburn, Kilmarnock, Scotland

ISBN - 13: 978-1-904064-49-7
ISBN - 10: 1-904064-49-3

40 Beansburn, Kilmarnock, Scotland

Typeset by John Ritchie Ltd., Kilmarnock
Printed by Bell & Bain Ltd., Glasgow

Contents

Foreword

This is my mother's story.

If you were to summarise my mother's life it would sound as if she was just one more victim of the tragedy that is the modern Middle East. Wadeah Habiby Musallam was born at the dawn of the 20th century and lived until the eve of the 21st. She survived two global conflicts, several civil wars and innumerable skirmishes. She lost her home and her country, was a refugee in a succession of nations and then lost her home once more. If that was not enough, she endured famine, illness, poverty, a broken marriage and widowhood with a family of four young girls. Yet my mother's long life was not one of tragedy but triumph and she was not a victim but a victor. She came to have a living faith in God and her confident testimony was that God kept her through it all.

From what I have just written, it would be easy to assume that my mother was someone who was, by nature, a saintly and teachable woman. That, as you will see, is not the case. By her own admission she was, in fact, a stubborn and rebellious soul whose will God had to break many times. My mother came to understand what *grace* means; that God can show persistent and repeated mercy on someone who does not deserve it. In one way my mother was a special person; yet in another she was a perfectly ordinary person in whose life an extraordinary God worked with extraordinary patience. God, not my mother, is the hero of this story; Wadeah would not want it any other way.

And that is, in its way, the simple lesson of my mother's life. God can be trusted in the worst and best of times.

I have written this account as if my mother was telling it. She was a born storyteller. Hers was almost the last generation who had only story telling to while away the candle lit evenings. After her came the electric light, the wireless, the television and the video; now the old stories – and the skill of telling them – are no more.

She told me her story, with her usual honesty and I now pass it on to you as she told me.

Siham Musallam Brown 2003

Acknowledgements

My gratitude to Chris Walley whose tireless and generous efforts helped to shape this biography.

Also to Thea Blackburn, Afaf Musallam, Roger Winson and Keith Pridden for their editing work and for transferring the manuscript to computer.

Not least to the number of friends whose reading of the manuscript and comments encouraged me on the way.

Siham Brown

CHAPTER 1

Early Memories

I was born on the 15th December 1907 in Shafa 'Amr in Lower Galilee, the fourth child and first daughter of Shukri and Wardeh Habiby. I was christened when I was a few days old and given the name Wadeah. Amongst Arabs, most of our personal names have meanings; Wadeah (pronounced Wad-i-yah) means 'meek and gentle of spirit'. As it turned it out, it was far from being an appropriate name.

The Shafa 'Amr of my childhood was a small village of pale stone houses near the brow of a hill. It was about ten miles from Haifa on the coast and about the same distance from Nazareth to the east. Shafa 'Amr was a mixed town; there were Moslems, Christians (both Catholics and Protestants), members of the Druze sect – that curious offshoot of Islam – and a handful of Jews. The groups were all quite distinct from one another in their beliefs and customs, but we tolerated one another with a generally polite self-control and in times of trouble (which were all too frequent), we rallied together.

Both my parents came from Protestant families. In the 19th century, many families from the older Christian denominations of the Middle East had become Protestants in our area. I never learned whether this is what happened with my ancestors, and if it was, what the details were; I just grew up knowing we were Protestants.

My grandfather Nakhleh Habiby was a wealthy landowner and when he died, his sons inherited his estate. My father gained more than his share of the estate: he was also offered the hand of his first cousin in marriage. She was still a baby! They were eventually married when she was fourteen and he was thirty. This was the sort of thing that happened in Shafa 'Amr where even by the end of 19th century, many of the customs hadn't changed since the days of the Bible. In spite of what might seem today as an unpromising start my parent's marriage was, despite its many trials, a long and happy one. They lived to celebrate their diamond-wedding anniversary and raised eleven children, nine of whom survived into adulthood.

Shukri, my father was a gentle and soft-spoken man from whom we rarely – if ever – had a harsh word. He was easy going and never seemed to demand much from life. Whatever the situation confronting him, he always faced it with a broad, gracious smile on his face. My father's pleasant manner, coupled with a handsome appearance – he had a fair complexion and blue eyes – had made him an attractive young man with a lot of charm.

My father and my mother had a simple faith and trust in God but it tended to get submerged under the burden of looking after the family. Given that the family eventually ran into double figures that burden was considerable.

Neither my father nor any of my brothers showed any interest in the land and because it was not registered legally, they gradually lost it all. Looking back on this, it is hard not to see the losses as being symbolic; foreshadowed the many other future losses they and we were to face. My father, no doubt aided by his charm, found a new job in teaching in the small village mission school that was run by the Church Missionary Society. There, in addition to teaching children, my father taught Arabic to British missionaries.

Despite his teaching role, my father knew very little English himself. He often told us an amusing story of how, while accompanying an English lady missionary from one village to another on horseback, he had realised it was getting late. The sun was heading for the horizon, she was riding very slowly and they were some way from the village. This posed a problem for my father; it would be quite improper for him and the woman to be seen together after nightfall. He tried to communicate his urgency but failed; she continued to ride at a slow pace. Finally, my father remembered an English sentence that he used to hear the schoolchildren chanting and, in desperation, called out, "Run, mouse run!" The message got through and the lady galloped onwards, with my father following, with no doubt, his broad smile beaming across his face.

It was in the Anglican missionary school at Shafa 'Amr that I had my first education. I was not, I confess, a keen scholar. I preferred roaming about in the fields and 'helping' the workers: that was much more fun. I saw no need for learning how to read and write, how to figure out numbers and, worst of all, how to keeping a thimble on the end of my middle finger during sewing lessons.

No, many things were far better than going to school. Best of all was visiting my numerous uncles and aunts. I loved Aunt Martha and her house the most. Its majestic rooms with their high vaulted ceilings were dark and cool and I would delight to follow my tall and beautiful aunt from one storeroom to another. I can see her now; her long black dress accentuating her height and her thick auburn hair plaited neatly into one golden braid which reached down to her waist. In my memory, it seems to me that my aunt's house was like a great cathedral and she was some sort of priest. And as she moved slowly through the storeroom, touching one sack of grain here and running her fingers through the contents of another, the autumn harvest smell would rise like incense and filled the room. Aunt Martha never seemed to be in a hurry and when she spoke to me or put me on her knee, I knew I could stay and listen to her as long as I wished. She had time for me.

But school remained. There though my mind was often a long way from the classroom. All too often the teachers would turn to me and ask 'Wadeah, do you understand?' Of course, I didn't and, amid a terribly drawn-out silence, the question would be repeated again and again. Once, in desperation, I answered 'yes' in a clear, ringing voice but I knew that my lie hadn't fooled the teacher.

To my young mind school was harsh and severe. Once when I did not hand in my homework, I was locked up in a small room. I began to cry out for Halim, one of my younger brothers.

'O Halim! Halim, my brother!' I wailed.

The teacher came rushing in. 'What's the matter? What's wrong with your brother, girl?' she asked, sounding very concerned. I brushed the tears off my face with the back of my hand and answered 'Nothing, I just feel I want to see him. I do miss him.' Turning her face away to hide her smile, the teacher let me out.

But Adib, another brother, did not get off so lightly. Adib had just completed his primary education at the village school and was waiting to start at the government intermediary school in Haifa. One day, while stopping by to see some of his friends who were still at school, he was caught fooling around with them in one of the classrooms. My brother slipped out quietly but the others were punished for their misdemeanour. A few days later, Miss Lawford, the headmistress, visited us and expressed a wish to see Adib at work. My father took her to the workshop where my brother, who was very interested in carpentry, spent most of his free time. Suddenly, without any explanation, Miss Lawford took hold of him and slapped his face two or three times. My father, who was standing nearby, was quite dumbfounded while my brother, who knew what it was all about, simply accepted his punishment silently. Then, without a word, Adib ushered Miss Lawford out of the house. As an inquisitive little girl just outside the workshop door, I saw everything and what I saw puzzled and bothered me. What was to turn out to be a long dislike of English missionaries had begun.

Looking back, I can see that I was little more than a small child yet already education, missionaries and Christianity had touched my life. How could I have known what role all three were to play in my future life?

One memory of my early years sticks in my mind very clearly. One day, word spread excitedly around the village that a small plane would be flying by over nearby fields that afternoon. It was the first plane ever in the area. It would fly low enough, they said, that anyone standing on the field would see the pilot inside.

As friends and neighbours from the village gathered, I found myself facing an irresistible temptation to try and get the best possible vantage point. I started to sneak away to where I thought I would get a better view.

"Wadeah!" my mother called to me as she saw what I was trying to do. "Stay here with everyone else, don't go wandering off on your own – it's too dangerous,"

But my mind was made up; whether it was dangerous or not, I was utterly determined to get the best view. I found a high spot and, standing on tiptoe on a ridge of ploughed earth, peered skyward. At last I saw the plane approaching from a distance like a silent bird, its wings catching the rays of the sun.

Suddenly it was upon us. Unprepared for the sudden noise or the speed of the plane as it swooped down over us, I fled. The next instant I found myself crouching for safety under the belly of a nearby donkey. To my embarrassment, I found out that I had been the only one who had not seen the pilot wave at us!

As I think about that story I see how, young as I was, my character was already there. I was already headstrong, imaginative and – above all – utterly determined to prove to my family, my friends and myself that I could stand up on my own two feet. Of course, growing up in the midst of eight brothers and a sister, there was no need for me to go looking for battles to fight; they were all around me. But the pattern was set; Wadeah Habiby was going to show everyone that she was independent; that she could enter the race and reach the goal on her own. And soon enough I added God to the list of those people from whom I wished to be independent.

Yet as I began my own private struggles, a greater and more public battle began. World War I started.

Most people now think of the First World War as having been fought almost entirely in Western Europe, yet there was also fighting around the eastern Mediterranean. Here, through ending the Ottoman Empire of the Turks, the First World War began a period of instability that has not yet ended. The Ottomans had ruled Palestine for four hundred years as part of an empire which, administered from Istanbul, extended from Eastern Europe to the Indian Ocean. Their once vigorous empire, had by 1914, become stale, bankrupt, corrupt and oppressive. It had been dying for many years and Turkey's decision to support Germany during the First World War was to turn out to be the fatal blow. What no one foresaw – least of all the Habibys of Shafa 'Amr – was how the death of the Ottoman Empire would start in motion events that would knock down everything we held dear.

At the beginning, the First World War – the Great War as it was called for many years – had very little effect on us. France and its trenches were a long way away; the nearest fighting to us was along the Suez Canal where the British forces in Egypt were defending their positions against the Turks. Increasingly though, there were dark rumours and worries in Palestine. But even as war threatened, a natural disaster struck us.

In the spring of 1915, our village and the surrounding region was struck by a vast plague of locusts. The summer harvest had just begun but only a few crops had been gathered and many late fruits such as figs and pomegranates were still on the trees and the bulk of the grain harvest was still standing in the fields. Out of nowhere, a black cloud floated down out of the sky and the locusts covered the land and the trees.

Slowly the cloud moved on and all that remained behind was tough grain stalks, half-dry leaves and the woody trunks and branches of the trees and, buried in the warm dry soil, millions of locust eggs. Our food supplies were drastically reduced and famine loomed.

Soon the eggs were hatching and the young locusts were on the move again. And while they couldn't fly, they could still eat. Anything green that had sprung up in the months since their parents had passed by was at risk. Fear gripped everyone's heart; rich and poor, old and young, Muslim and Christian: all were afraid. They had already suffered enough.

The Turkish government had an inspiration – they called on all the villagers to get out into the fields and gather the locusts with their hands and place them in large sacks. As an encouragement, a small sum of money was paid for every sack full of locusts that was collected. I went out with my family and we did our share in rounding up the horrid creatures. To this day, I still shiver when I think of how I picked up those struggling things in my hands. For a long time everyone went without their daily bread but finally our combined fight against the locusts was successful.

Now, though, the war overtook the locusts as our main concern. In 1917, the British forces under General Allenby began to advance into Palestine. By early December of that year, Jerusalem had been taken by the British and the Turks were retreating northwards. By the very end of the year, Jaffa had fallen and the British were only seventy miles away from Shafa 'Amr. For the first time in my life – but sadly not the last – I heard the rumblings of distant guns.

The war suddenly began to raise many urgent questions. How would the war affect the missionaries, the school and the church? After all, our church school was run by British missionaries! What were we going to do? The questions were unanswered.

Soon Turkish soldiers with guns began wearily climbing the hill road to Shafa 'Amr and taking up positions. The missionaries were ordered by their embassies to pack and leave; many of them – the optimists – going only as far as Egypt. The school was closed down and, after bitter arguments between the Church Missionary Society and the local church synod, the church was closed as well. This annoyed the residents since they felt that there was an understanding that the church would not close its doors under any circumstances as long as there was a priest to minister to the people. Sadly, the Turkish soldiers had no respect for mission decisions, rules, or for people's wishes. They forced their way into the church, desecrating it and used it for their headquarters.

The arrival of the Turkish Army in Shafa 'Amr resulted in new problems for the Habiby family. The Ottoman Empire was now fighting for its survival in the Middle East and their leaders knew it; desperately short of manpower, the Turks started conscripting local men into their army. As they did, every young man of an age suitable for military service vanished overnight; disappearing off the roads, from their homes and their places of work. Many were rounded up but some managed to slip out of our village under cover of night and, eventually, out of Palestine altogether.

With eight boys, it was inevitable that our family would have someone of suitable age. My eldest brother Wadii fled, and aided by the sale of some of my mother's jewellery, reached Cairo safely. There he sought, and received, an uncle's help in finding some employment. Because he had been educated at Bishop Gobat School in Sahyoun, Jerusalem, Wadii's English was very good and as a result, he was given a job as an interpreter in the British Army. Adib, the second eldest son – the one who had been punished by Miss Lawford – was however, not so fortunate. He was caught by the Turks and served as a reluctant soldier for them under incredibly harsh conditions. He deserted twice. The first time he crept home in the middle of the night on his hands and knees, barefoot, with a torn uniform, encrusted with dirt and mud and crawling with lice. He was so weak with hunger and exhaustion that he was unable to stand upright. Silently, we younger children were shepherded out of our bedroom and put together in our mother's bed while she and my father tended to Adib. Water was heated in the kitchen, and with some assistance, my brother was able to get washed and cleaned up. Then, with some hot food inside him, he slept the remainder of the night and much of the following two days.

Unfortunately, despite my mother finding ingenious ways of hiding him, Adib was eventually tracked down by the Turks. He was returned to the Ottoman army and punished for desertion but fortunately, he was spared being shot. In the months that followed, he suffered from typhus, hunger and more ill-treatment. He deserted again, but was caught before reaching home and returned to his army unit. Again, he was spared the death penalty.

After the speed of the British advance in 1917, everyone expected that they would continue to move northwards. In fact, it was not to be. We didn't realise it at the time but the situation in France was so desperate for the Allies by early 1918 that half of Allenby's army was shipped off to fight there. So, unaware that the British had no intention of advancing, we spent the first half of 1918 under a nervous expectation that any day the fighting would engulf us.

The final twelve months of the war were grim for everybody and, ever afterwards, the memories of it were those of hunger, weariness and hopelessness. The older men lost their jobs, and those young men who were not conscripted had no work to which to go. The storerooms, which had never recovered from the plague of locusts, were now raided by the Turks to feed their men. There was the land, of course, but that needed time to produce and yield food.

For the Habiby family too, life was miserable. Wadie was in Egypt and Adid, an unenthusiastic soldier for the Ottomans. The only food we had was what could grow on the land and we often went hungry. There was no sugar, no kerosene for cooking, no soap for washing and worst of all, very little salt to be had.

The salt shortage could, however with difficulty be resolved as the sea was only ten miles away. But it meant hard work. It became the women's task to take the donkeys to the beach by night and load sackfuls of salty sand on the backs of the animals. On arriving home, the sand was soaked in water to produce brine which was then boiled or evaporated away to produce tiny quantities of precious salt. It all sounded very exciting and grown-up to me.

I had to be involved. I insisted on accompanying my mother and the other women on a trip to collect salt. They tried to reason with me but I was too obstinate to be convinced. My stubborn will was manifesting itself again!

We set off and, riding part of the way, I found the trip down to the coast enjoyable. But the journey back was a very different matter. Because the donkeys were now burdened with the sand, I could not ride and had instead to walk all the way. It was too much for my little legs and I soon began to fall behind. I became aware that the women were ahead of me and that I could not keep up with them. My mother seemed to have taken it for granted that I was following close behind. In the darkness my heart began to be suddenly filled with every childish fear and horror, real and imaginary. Yet amid the fear, I was also aware that I was exhausted and that sleep was starting to creep over me. Even though I was walking, I could not keep my eyes open. Fighting off both fear and exhaustion, I ran to the nearest donkey and grabbed hold of its tail.

Somehow – did I sleep-walk? – I finally made it home. But I had learnt my lesson. I made no further journeys with my mother for salt again.

Somehow, in spite of my mother's constant hard work both in the house and in the fields, she often found the time and the energy to gather us children together and tell us stories from the Bible. On occasions, she would read us, in her hesitant way, a short passage from the Bible. Having been married at fourteen, my mother had had only elementary education and her ability at reading was not great.

One evening, just before the end of the war, she read us the story of Jephthah (Judges 1:30-40). I was gripped by this man's story and, in particular, his vow that, if he returned victorious from the war, he would sacrifice the first creature that he set eyes on. The story particularly impressed me because, in this time of desperation, people all around me were making vows and promises to God about what they would do for him if he would only bring the war to an end. I had felt that I too wanted to make a vow but felt that I had nothing to offer to God. Now though I realised that I could, like Jephthah, make a vow to offer a sacrifice.

The following evening I stood alone at sunset in the field next to our house, and prayed to God. "Please God,' I said, "if you will stop this war and bring my two brothers back home safely I will give you..." The next words came naturally, "...myself as a sacrifice."

I have often wondered what I really meant by my vow. I am sure, that I genuinely and sincerely meant every word I said. But I am also sure that I had not stopped to think how, if God fulfilled his part of the bargain, I would fulfil mine.

Finally, though, the war did end. In September 1918, the British forces under Allenby went on the offensive against a demoralised Turkish Army. On September 19th, the Turks were thoroughly defeated at the Battle of Megiddo and Allenby's cavalry raced northwards. Within days the Turkish Army had melted away, pulling out of Shafa 'Amr and many other parts of Palestine. In late October 1918, with their army pushed out of Palestine and Syria, the Turkish Army surrendered. The long Ottoman rule had come to an end.

What we didn't realise then was that, as part of their efforts to get rid of the Ottomans, the British had made a number of secret promises. The British promised the Arabs independence if they would rebel against the Ottomans, which they duly did. The British made a second agreement with the French and Russians to divide the entire Middle East into areas of influence. And finally, the British made a third commitment; they promised prominent British Jews that they would support a Jewish homeland in Palestine. The three promises were of course, contradictory and even as the Ottomans were retreating, the stage was being set for further disaster.

But, perhaps thankfully, in Shafa 'Amr we knew nothing of all this. It was enough that the war was over. There was little celebration: people were too weary to make merry over someone else's victory or even rejoice in their oppressor's defeat. Yet, amidst the weariness, there was – at last – hope in the air. Peace and plenty were on our doorstep at last. And I had the joy of knowing that my two older brothers were safe. Adib, released by the collapse of the Turkish Army, had lost no time in coming home. Soon news came that Wadii was returning from Egypt and preparations were made to meet him at the port in Haifa and to bring him home.

In fact, Wadii had not simply survived, he had done very well for himself. He had a well-paid and secure job with the British government in Egypt and had decided to come home and visit the family in Shafa 'Amr. The day of his arrival at the port arrived and my father hired a large horse-drawn bus that soon filled up with family and friends as we journeyed to Haifa. On the way, there was singing and clapping, and sweets and food were shared around. Happy and contented smiles were on every face and, at least for the time being, the war and all its pain were forgotten.

The port in Haifa made an unforgettable impression on my little eleven-year-old mind. Compared to the tranquillity of Shafa 'Amr, it was a scene of extraordinary busyness and noise. There were ships unloading goods and people, the banging and clanging of cargo, the cries and bustle of departures and arrivals. The sun enveloped all with a hazy shimmer and the salty smell of the sea gave flavour and taste to the picture. I stared around, my eyes suddenly opening to a vast new world beyond my little village. It was a world that I found almost overwhelmingly attractive. I knew then that I wanted to be part of this world with its fresh, varied sounds, smells and sights. In my innocent naivety, this newly discovered world charmed me and I saw nothing in it to frighten or alarm me. How little I knew or understood then!

Suddenly Wadii's voice broke my reverie. Strong, handsome and full of bubbling laughter he engulfed me in his arms with a bear-like hug and then stepped back to review the effect of nature and the passage of time on me. He seemed to approve and I took his pleased look and pat on my shoulder to mean that I had passed his scrutiny. He looked well to me and I felt that the Egyptian accent his Arabic had acquired suited him. Everything about him made him seem very special in my eyes.

Karim, my third brother spoiled the last part of the journey home for me. He had planned to bring two horses from Haifa back to the village with him but, like everyone else, he wanted to be on the coach with his returning brother. So he asked me to bring the horses home by riding one and leading the second after me.

My refusal was adamant. I told Karim that there was no way that I would do what he wanted. No kind words, bribes or threats could force me to take those two horses home alone. I too, wanted to be on the coach. In the end, neither of us got to be on the coach. Somehow, it was sorted out that we took a horse each and rode back together on a side road. Karim was so furious with me that our journey home was interrupted by him constantly teasing me and aiming half-hearted blows at me.

In hindsight, I can see yet here another sign of my stubbornness; my will was already becoming as hard as flint.

Within a short period of time life returned to normal. Palestine became ruled by the British rather than the Turks but little changed in Shafa 'Amr. Father opened a small grocery shop in the village and schools reopened. Soon we heard to our pleasure that the British were transferring Wadii back to Palestine from Egypt and he was going to Haifa.

Adib, ever the woodworker, was now working in the railways in Haifa as a carpenter. Karim was already seriously thinking of moving his taxi business to the city; he already had two horse-drawn carriages in use. It was hardly surprising therefore that the whole family decided to move to Haifa. I, of course, was delighted.

And my vow? I had forgotten it.

CHAPTER 2

Haifa

1920 - 1922

I had great dreams and high expectations of life in Haifa and I was not disappointed.

You might think that, after living in our little village, we would have found the big town of Haifa unfriendly but that was not the case. My three older brothers were already well established in their various businesses there and they, and others who had moved to Haifa before us, were welcoming, protective, and full of advice and warnings. We found ourselves amongst many friends, relatives and neighbours. Although we were now in the big town, it seemed as if we were still part of a village.

My two younger brothers, Halim and Nakhleh, were sent to the local school and it was soon my turn to follow them. It was a prospect that aroused mixed feelings in me. One part of me was excited at the idea of starting a new school while another part was rather apprehensive. I was very much a country girl and was unsure how I would settle in. I had reached thirteen and was already tall; I stood out among other girls of my age. The combination of my height and my country upbringing sharpened the self-consciousness of adolescence so that I was almost painfully aware of myself. I knew that I smiled shyly, that I tilted my head sideways when spoken to, that I moved with a slow (and I hoped) graceful gait, that my voice was soft and gentle and that my words never came out harshly. But I was all too aware that I stuck out among my peers as being different and out of place.

My fear that I would not fit in had some basis. My new classmates in Haifa did not appreciate me. I was an outsider. They found me too gentle and too naïve: I failed to understand their jokes and I found their humour unsavoury. I decided that our move to the city had taken place a little too late; our family seemed too slow in climbing up the social ladder. I felt everyone was one rung above us, and me in particular. It was not a situation I enjoyed.

My new school was much more formal than the one I had attended in Shafa 'Amr; here in Haifa the whole business of teaching and education was taken more seriously. Yet perhaps strangely, I found that I enjoyed school life. Looking back, I can see that my new interest in learning was partly a response to the better teaching but it was also because my pride and desire for independence were reasserting themselves. Learning offered me a way in which I could advance and make progress ahead of others. If I could not join my peers, then I could perhaps beat them.

There were however, troubling issues at home at this time. One of them centred on my relationship with my sister, Aniseh. Aniseh was just a year younger than I was and we were, perhaps, too close for comfort. Aniseh, a much stronger character than I was, tended to get her own way. Much quieter, I tended to accept things as they were. Yet my acceptance was superficial: there was always an inner resentment. My problems with Aniseh were heightened because I felt that she was much prettier too. Slowly, these hidden emotions built up inside me and began to seep out as expressions of jealousy and hatred against my sister. Sadly, our struggles were not just private and mental ones: they often flared up in angry words or blows. The fighting solved nothing but simply left a legacy of bitterness that compounded our mutual dislike.

Another problem was that life at home became very busy and soon began to encroach on my blossoming school career. We found ourselves moving house in order that the whole family could live together again. Within a short time of us coming to Haifa two more boys, Emile and Naim, were born and then a new baby sister – Nada. On the edge of becoming a teenager, I took particular interest in my new brothers and sister. Soon, with my mother's increased load of housework, these three new additions to the family became my special responsibility. I found myself looking after them and loving them as if they were my own. Even to this day, a very special bond of affection still exists between us.

At the time, the house we lived in was almost opposite my school and its proximity was to have a direct effect on my future. My mother – overstretched by all her responsibilities – soon found it all too convenient to call me from school or keep me at home after lunch break. The requests were soon all too familiar: 'Wadeah, could you just keep an eye on your sick brother, while I do the shopping' or 'Wadeah, please just take this parcel down to the shop, your father is waiting for it'. The list was endless. Very soon, the frequency of my absences had been noted by the school authorities.

I was saddened and embarrassed to lose so much schooling but I could see no solution to my problem. Finally, close to my fourteenth birthday, one of my teachers, Mrs Nucho, took me aside one day and had a chat. Mrs Nucho knew our family slightly; she was not only a very capable teacher but also a caring and understanding person. As she listened to my problems, I felt that she had sensed in me the desire I had to continue with my education and had recognised the impossible situation that I faced at home.

After our conversation, Mrs Nucho spoke to my parents. She raised the possibility of me getting a place in the Bethlehem branch of the CMS School. Would they give their consent to my going as a boarder? My parents thanked Mrs Nucho for her concern and interest in my education and well-being and agreed that I could go. It must have been a great sacrifice for my mother: she had become increasingly dependent on having me at home to look after her youngest three children.

I soon received news that I was accepted at the Bethlehem school. In fact, I had more than an acceptance; there was also a promise with it that, in two years time when I was sixteen, I would have the option to do a teacher's training course.

In an instant, the path of my life seemed settled. Becoming a teacher would, I decided there and then, be an excellent choice for my future career. I quickly convinced myself that, with Mrs. Nucho as my model, teaching would be the answer to my search to attain my own place in society. As a teacher, Wadeah Habiby could be a person in her own right.

Yet as I considered the wonderful new opportunity that now stretched out before me, I suddenly realised that I would miss my family desperately. My links with the youngest three members of our family were already deep. My heart went out to Emile, Naim and Nada and suddenly the thought of leaving them seemed like an act of desertion. With me gone, who would help the boys with their homework and see that their school clothes and Sunday suits and shirts were always clean and ready? And would Mother have the time to look after baby Nada, as I did? Would she brush her silky brown hair every morning and tie a brightly coloured ribbon round it? Would Mother manage to ensure that she has a clean dress on every day? I had my doubts.

As I thought about how I would miss them, another

question arose to torment me: would they miss me? When I had been Nada's age and had no sister to play with I had invented an imaginary playmate to share the day; would she now do the same?

I ran to the three infants, with hugs and kisses and tears streaming down my face, told them my news, and assured them that I would never forget them. I promised them that there would be presents every time I came home. I would write as well, I told them; well at least from time to time. But they in turn, I said, would have to write back and tell me their news and that of the whole family. At the time, there was one particular bit of news that I was specially anxious not to miss; my two older brothers were courting.

That summer I found myself frequently sitting down with my mother and watching her as she sewed my dresses for school and prepared clothes and the other requirements I had. I realised that I had never been really close to my mother. She had always been so busy that all she had ever been able to give us children was our food and clothing; there had never been any time for any real conversation or any interchange of ideas or opinions. Now though on the verge of leaving home, I felt drawn to her in a special way and wished that she would respond. Yet as I voiced my choice on my clothing, my comments would be met with only a momentary far-away glimmer of interest on my mother's face. Then the interest would soon melt away and she would say something such as: 'Wadeah, these clothes will do, there's nothing wrong with them.'

Then tragedy struck. Aniseh suddenly became very ill as a result of sunstroke. In a moment, all my envy and hatred of my sister melted away and instead, heart-rending remorse set in. I prayed desperately. I told God that if only he would give her back to me I would never fight with her or hit her again. I promised him that I would love her. I pleaded that if she lived, I would put my arms around her and say, 'Sweet sister Aniseh, please forgive me for all the times I hurt you and made life difficult for you.' If she lived.

But she didn't. My prayers were not answered and aged just twelve, my sister died.

With Aniseh's death, my mother experienced a silent, helpless sorrow. Somehow accepting the terrible event that had happened made me one with her. For the first time, I felt my mother and I were close. It was as if my sister's death had brought us together.

Slowly, I somehow learnt to accept Aniseh's death too. But in that time of awesome, mysterious mourning, I remembered the vow I had made to God about my brothers. I realised that I could have lost them as easily as I had lost Aniseh. And as I remembered my vow, I realised that it needed to be repaid. But would I ever know how to pay God back what I owed him?

The remaining summer months saw us in constant activity. Summers were always busy times but this year we were even busier. I can see now that, in order to try to forget our grief, as a family we chose to throw ourselves into our activities. I became whole-heartedly involved in the preparation of food for the winter months.

One summer activity was preserving tomatoes by making them into a concentrated puree, which could be used in cooking during the winter months when fresh tomatoes were not in season. Making the puree involved straining tomato juice, then boiling the juice with salt until most of the water had evaporated and then what was left was reduced to the consistency of a thick sauce. The sauce was then poured in large flat dishes or specially made shallow trays and then left in the sun for a few days until it became a thick dark red puree which was put in jars and sealed. It was hard work. Friends and relatives all helped and we children did what we could. But we all knew that the one who worked hardest was my mother.

One thing that had to be made in summer was *burghul* or cracked wheat. To make *burghul*, you had to wash the wheat, boil it and then let it dry in the sun on the rooftop, before sending it to the mill for grinding. Ground fine, *burghul* was used in dishes such as *tabbouleh* (a finely chopped tomato, mint and parsley salad) and *kubbeh* (a fried minced lamb); ground coarse, it was used for cooking with meat. To make enough *burghul* for our family, we needed many sacks of wheat. Large clean white sheets were spread on the rooftop of the house. In the back yard, a temporary outdoor cooking fire was set up – a few bricks arranged in a semi-circular fashion with small pieces of heavy logs in the centre and on top of the bricks sat a large copper tub half filled with water. When the burning wood had brought the water to the boil, the wheat grain was poured into the water and left to cook until it was tender. Then with large, long handled perforated ladles the swollen cooked grain was lifted out of the copper tub, put in large baskets and taken up to the roof. There, it was spread out on the sheets and left for two to three days to dry out completely. We children helped in the last two stages and, as a reward, each of us received a bowl of the still hot wheat mixed with sugar, raisins, nuts and spices.

Those evenings are fixed in my memory. I remember how we would gather round the dying fire as the tub was removed and the sun set into the Mediterranean. There, tired and hungry, we would savour our well-earned food as we watched the dying embers. Every now and then, a thin streak of flame would come to life and leap upwards as the breeze gently fanned the heat away. Finally, the embers and the sunset would fade away and it was time for bed.

Within a few weeks, my mother had me all ready and equipped for boarding school. For the first time in my life, mother seemed to show a real personal interest in me and my affairs. My departure seemed to bring a special joy and happiness yet when the day came for me to leave, there were tears in both my parents' eyes.

I left for Bethlehem assured that I had their blessing but also painfully aware how much my departure hurt them.

CHAPTER 3

Bethlehem

1922 - 1924

A small country bus took me from Haifa to Bethlehem. As we left the coast and began to climb, I felt the air becoming cooler; here up on the hills of Palestine, autumn seemed already imminent. Finally, on the slope of a hill just above the centre of Bethlehem, the bus stopped outside a gate on which three large interwoven brass letters gleamed in the sun: *BGS*. I had arrived at Bethlehem Girls School.

As the bus drove away down towards the town of Bethlehem, I stood there staring at the place that was to be my home for at least two years. A potpourri of emotions engulfed me; all at once, I seemed to feel youthful excitement, the tang of adventure, and the bitterness of homesickness. Finally, I took a firm grasp of my suitcase, lifted it and with determined resolution, walked towards the main school building.

At the door I was met by a welcoming lady who helped me in with my luggage and then led me to the registration room. There my name, address and other vital pieces of information were recorded before I was introduced to the headmistress, Miss Miller. She was a tall woman who somehow combined a rather distant and austere manner with a kindly face. She welcomed me to the school and expressed the hope that I would be happy and that I would make good use of my time. Then suddenly, she gave me a stiff nod and a smile and I realised that my interview was ended.

A lady who, I was told, was my 'dormitory mother' led me

towards the dormitories; I had little idea what her title meant and it gave me little comfort. Together, we walked along the corridors, our footsteps ringing and echoing on the scrubbed white stone floors. I struggled not to be overwhelmed by the bleak and sterile atmosphere that enveloped me: my home seemed infinitely far away. From the various rooms came sounds of laughter and loud, excited, girlish babbling.

Finally, we came to a door, my escort stopped and, opening the door, ushered me in. My first impression was of a long and narrow room, with beds alternating with small cabinets and chairs down both sides and curious faces turned towards me. 'Wadeah Habiby' said a voice, as if from a distance and I suddenly realized that my dormitory mother was introducing me to the girls. It turned out that two of them, Nadia Kamaze and Souad Nassar, were newcomers like me, and they made me feel at ease. As it turned out, I was to become good friends with Nadia and Souad and we were to have great times together.

The girls were friendly and soon made me feel at ease. In fact, settling at BGS turned out to be a much smoother process than I had anticipated. Most of the girls were pleasant and I quickly made good friends. Socially, I still felt ill at ease but somehow it seemed to be much less of a problem here than in Haifa.

As in my previous school, teaching at BGS was a serious and formal business and it seemed to be assumed that every girl would make good academic progress. Yet as Miss Miller reminded us, academic progress was not enough: we were also to achieve goals in social awareness and etiquette.

Of course, being at a boarding school meant that there was a lot more than studying to be done. There was always housework, such as scrubbing the stone floors on our hands and knees. Slowly – and reluctantly – I adjusted to having my freedom limited. I felt confined by the school and my time seemed organised by bells. There were, it seemed, bells from the moment of waking up until the time when we scrambled into our beds at night and lights were turned off.

Accustomed as I was to the mild weather of the coast I found the first winter at the school hard and struggled to keep warm. Bethlehem experienced a severe climate and school, set high on the hillside and exposed to the elements seemed particularly prone to biting frosty winds. Sadly, just how cold it could get was memorably demonstrated by the fate of Biddeesh, our pet goat. Biddeesh had originally been bought for the Girl Guides to practice animal care and management but had ended up as the school mascot. Her unusual name had been given to her as a rather heavy-handed reminder to us to be obedient and willing. *Biddeesh* is colloquial Arabic for 'I don't want to' a phrase that we were not expected to use in school. So if, in a moment of obstinacy or wilfulness any of us said 'I don't want to' the stern response was automatic; '*Biddeesh* is in the hut!' Biddeesh spent the day foraging on the hillsides and on cold nights was brought in to a small garden storeroom where she had sweet hay for food and a dry straw bed to sleep on. One frosty winter evening the girls who were responsible for Biddesh that week forgot to bring her in for the night and the next morning the goat was found frozen to death on the frost-covered slopes.

Inevitably, at a school run by the Anglican missionaries, Christian teaching was very prominent. Yet here it had a meaning that I had never seen in Shafa 'Amr. The Bible was not just taught: it was lived out in the lives of the missionaries and local teachers. My childhood fears and doubts raised by the inconsistencies I had sensed at my village school began to wane as I lived amongst Christians who were kind, loving, fair and forgiving. As it happened, this last quality was soon put to the test. In a moment of childishness, my friend Nadia and I decided to investigate the theory that blind people possessed an extra-sensory ability of being able to feel the presence of another person near them. There was an obvious subject for the experiment: Miss Adaille Dafesh, our Scripture and music teacher who was totally blind. One day, we were already standing on the path through the cloisters when we saw her coming towards us. Miss Dafesh knew the school premises so well she hardly ever used her white stick and on this occasion walked confidently with her head held up high and carrying an armful of music sheets. Nadia and I glanced at each other, and then stood silent and motionless on the path. Miss Dafesh came to within a couple of yards from where we were standing then suddenly, without slowing her pace, moved slightly to the left as though to avoid us.

There was a crunching noise as her face hit the pillar to her left and her dark glasses and music sheets flew to the ground. She stopped dead still. Racked with guilt, Nadia and I rushed to her assistance and with a grieved embarrassment explained our cruel experiment and asked her forgiveness. Without a word, Miss Dafesh stiffly nodded towards us, stuck the music sheets we had offered her back under an arm, put the dark glasses back on her face and with her free hand protecting her bruised nose, continued on her way. For several days, Nadia and I waited in a painful expectancy for a summons to the Principal's office. Yet the call to see Miss Miller never came. Miss Dafesh had forgiven us and, as far as I know, she never told a soul about us.

Sundays were exciting days and gave us a glimpse of another world. The school was within walking distance of the centre of Bethlehem with its Manger Square and the Basilica of the Nativity. After breakfast, we had only the bare minimum of housework to do and then in our smart navy Sunday uniform we took the short walk to the Anglican Church in Bethlehem. In an orderly fashion we would walk together down the drive and pass through the school gates; a moment that always gave me an extraordinary sense of freedom. After a short distance walk along the main road, we would turn off onto a footpath across a small field and then, with a brief final walk along a single narrow cobbled stone street we would be there. Beneath the imposing arched doorway of the church, gigantic doors would already be pushed back open on their shiny brass hinges. The minister in his priestly gown would stand to one side, wish us good morning and then show us and our teachers to our assigned pews. As we usually arrived before the rest of the congregation, we had the opportunity of watching and observing the pious folk of Bethlehem and the surrounding area as they entered and sat in their family pews.

Some of the wealthiest and noblest of Palestinian families were found in Bethlehem, Beit Jala and the surrounding area and the Sunday service gave them an opportunity to show off. It was a splendid and unforgettable spectacle. I watched the women most: to me they seemed tall and elegant and many of them had fair hair and complexions. They wore their very best clothes and as they walked elegantly past us, we could smell the amber and sandalwood of the chests where these clothes had been kept during the week. The ladies of Bethlehem were famous for their embroidery and their Sunday finery displayed their skills with colourful cross-stitch down the front of their dresses and round the hem. On their heads they had a pure white muslin headdress which came down over their shoulders and back ending in triangle of fabric below their waists. On the fold across the brow there would be a string of gold and silver coins threaded in an overlapping fashion which caught and reflected the flicker of the church candle flames or the outdoor sunshine. When they stood beside their black-suited husbands and their children with their brightly coloured clothes, the effect was so striking that I could hardly keep my eyes away from them

Many of these women were renowned for their culinary skills and on a number of occasions we were invited to different families for Sunday lunch. We felt tremendously honoured to attend these sumptuous feasts, where we were pressed to eat so much that you might have thought that we were having our last meal on earth. I can still hear a presiding matron saying again and again, in the special Bethlehem singsong dialect, 'Sisters, have some more: we eat every day.'

So winter passed into spring and the heat of summer began. Sooner than I could have imagined, my first year at Bethlehem Girls School drew to a close and I found myself back at home with my family. Now almost sixteen, I was aware how much I had matured. I had discovered responsibility at school and found it both desirable and enjoyable. I felt I was a grown up now — not because others treated me as one, but simply because I knew I was one. I had also acquired knowledge and already discovered the answers to many questions that puzzled me as a child. My younger brothers and my sister admired my views and opinions, my older brothers treated me with respect and my mother and father were proud of me. At last, I felt I was an equal. My newfound self-confidence was such that I felt deeply insulted when, at the end of the holidays, my brother Karim saw me to the bus to Bethlehem and urged the bus driver to make sure I got to school safely

One burdensome question that I had neither forgotten nor answered was my childhood vow to God. How, where and when did I offer a sacrifice – myself – to God? If I promised to do something for him or give something to him, what would it be? The answer came one Sunday evening at school when a visiting missionary spoke to us about Christian commitment and offering ourselves to serve the Lord. Those two words 'offering' and 'serving' filled my heart and mind with a strange joy of certainty. I felt the assurance of recognition; it was as if I had suddenly arrived at a place for which I had long sought. Filled with the peace of a problem solved and a burden lifted I heard nothing else that was said after those words. When at the end of the talk, there was an invitation given to come forward 'if the Lord had spoken to us', I was the first to go to the front of the hall. A few others followed too. Of course, I did not really understand the meaning of commitment or the significance of what Christ had done for me. All I knew was that God had answered a childhood request of mine and he had kept my brothers safe during the war and now I'd discovered the way to God. That way was through a commitment to offer myself to him in 'serving'.

After the service, Miss Miller the headmistress called me and another girl who had also stood up to see her in her office. 'How do we serve God?' was the question uppermost in my mind. The answer, I was told, was 'to become a missionary'. There were other questions: Would I be prepared to travel and live far away from home? Would I be willing to love people who spoke a strange language and learn their language too? Would I be willing to bear the heat and any other form of discomfort that I was faced with? To all these I answered 'Yes'.

I kept these – and many other– questions in my heart and thought about them on my own later. I was quite certain God had called me to serve him. China seemed to be my destination, for no better reason than that our missionary speaker was a member of CMS and had worked in China. I was also aware that my family would do everything in their power to stop me. However, as I planned to have two more years at school in order to do teacher training, that was not a battle that I had to face immediately. I felt that I would rather face them with my decision at the last possible moment. By then I would be almost eighteen and far more able to stand up for my rights.

Having made my commitment, I now began the task of preparing myself. One way was for me to read God's word and to spend time in prayer. Another way of preparation came through the headmistress, through whom I was given special responsibilities and minor jobs to do at school. Whether I was looking after a group of the younger girls at school, arranging the guest room for some visitors or accompanying Miss Dafesh as she taught Braille in the nearby villages of Beit Jala and Beit Sahur, it all amounted to one thing — serving the Lord. That was enough to give me joy and satisfaction.

Suddenly, it all ended. In the third term of that second

year, we were abruptly told that school was to be closed in the immediate future. The bad news came like a thunderbolt from a perfectly blue sky. The headmistress, Miss Miller, came back from an executive meeting in Jerusalem at the CMS Field Headquarters and immediately called a staff meeting, told the staff and then informed the whole school. The reason for the closure was that there was a great need to open an orphanage in Nazareth and the CMS could not at that time support both our school in Bethlehem and the new home in Nazareth. Our school was a charitable organisation and therefore a drain on mission resources. It was argued that it was not unreasonable to expect the girls who attended BGS to go instead to day schools in their own towns and cities. So that was that.

We were given letters for our parents explaining the situation and offering suggestions of help and advice on what schools to approach so that we could complete our final two years. It was a time of overwhelming sadness for me: my hopes and plans had focussed on the school and with the news of its impending closure; they threatened to crumble away entirely. I had a deep fear that once I got home, I would stay there. I had already had more schooling than many girls of my age and I felt there was a real danger that my parents would say that I had had enough. If that happened I would have suddenly reached the end of a road that had promised to lead somewhere, at least to my independence. And there was my intention of serving God as a missionary. Didn't he want my offer? Wasn't it, perhaps, good enough?

I felt very small, alone and weak. I had believed that I was a confident adult yet now, faced with a major problem for the first time, my confidence had suddenly slipped away exposing the child within. Once more I was a little village girl lost in the city of life. I now found that my experience of Christianity seemed to be little comfort: I now saw my faith as something remote and inapplicable. I sensed that I had tried to do a kind of a business deal with God and that whatever had happened to me was no more than a superficial experience. My heart had been involved and I did not really know God. In fact, in the crisis that I found myself passing through didn't even think of approaching Him for help. I saw it as my problem, and mine alone.

The last few weeks at school flew by as if in a dream. To any outside observer, our school life would have seemed as usual. Like some deep, smooth river the combination of discipline, routine and the habit of working to schedules carried us unstoppably through to the end of term.

Once more, but now for the last time, an assortment of suitcases, trunks and bags stood outside the main gate waiting to be picked up by their owners. It was with great difficulty that tears were kept in check as goodbyes were said and promises made to write and keep in touch. But once I was in my seat on the Haifa bus, I found that there was no holding back my gushing stream of tears and half-stifled sobs. I turned my head firmly towards the window to escape being noticed by other passengers. Through my tears I caught a glimpse of my own reflection in the glass – a sad little face with large, puzzled moist eyes. The sight was so pitiable that my heart was filled with a wave of sympathy for myself and I shed new fresh tears.

So I left Bethlehem Girls School. What happened to the school? A group of wealthy local people bought the school with the intention of renovating and modernising it and then opening it up as fee-paying day school for girls. The staff though all went to Bir Zeit and under the directorship of Nabiha Nasser started Bir Zeit College in 1924.

In fact, although I knew little about them (and cared even less) there were more dramatic and ominous issues emerging in Palestine than the closure of a girl's school. Part of the legacy of the Great War was that Palestine had fallen under the British Mandate. While supposed to be helping the Arabs gain independence, the British had also made a commitment to aiding the formation of a Jewish homeland in Palestine.

As part of that commitment, they encouraged Jewish immigration to Palestine. Somehow, the British seem to have believed that a Jewish homeland and a self-governing Arab population could coexist. How hopelessly naïve this was, soon became apparent.

There had always been a small Jewish population in Palestine which had traditionally enjoyed good relations with the Arabs, whether Moslems or Christians. All this now changed. Part of the issue was numbers: from 1920 the size of the Jewish population began to rise rapidly as immigration to Palestine began. Matters made worse by the fact that many of the Jewish immigrants were wealthier than the Arabs; something that inevitably aroused resentment. Aggravating the situation still further was the fact that many of the new arrivals were uncompromising Zionists; they believed Palestine was theirs and theirs alone. The result was a growing tension between once tolerant communities and as early as 1920 there were riots between Jews and Arabs. They were a small, grim foreshadowing of what was to come. For a number of years there were no more major riots but the tension between the communities never waned and suspicion bred more suspicion.

But Wadeah Habiby had problems of her own.

CHAPTER 4

Nursing Training

1924 - 1932

Back home, I joined in the usual social and household activities of the summer with my family and waited to see what my parents would decide. Finally, I learned that they had decided to send me to something that was called the English High School in Haifa. A church school rather than a missionary school, it was highly thought of as an academic institution that drew its students from among the most superior families of Haifa society. I was willing to give it a try and went there dressed from head to toe in full school uniform. One day was all that it took for me to know, without a shadow of a doubt, that it wasn't for me. I soon told my parents that I would not return there for the second term and they knew that I meant it. My mother's response was 'Very well, Wadeah, you stay at home, there's plenty to do here. We need you.'

Her comments focussed my attention on my future. I had no desire to stay at home. Under the British Mandate, Palestine was changing but in the mid 1920s it was still not common for a girl to go out to work. If their families allowed them to work, two professions were more or less acceptable for women; these were teaching and nursing. Of these, teaching was the most respectable: there was something much less honourable about nursing.

I soon decided that I would become a nurse. My decision

was not just a sudden or passing whim. As a child, I had always imagined myself a nurse and in playing with other children, it was always me who bandaged them up, took their temperature and gave them their injections. But would my parents approve a career of nursing? It was something that couldn't be taken for granted and I decided that in order to achieve what I wanted I would have to plan my campaign very carefully. One wrong step and I would have lost the battle completely and be sentenced to stay at home.

I started with my brothers. If they could be won to my side, I could count on their support when I faced my father. Only four of my brothers really mattered: the three who were older than me (Wadii, Adib and Karim) and Halim, who was a year younger than I was. I approached them one by one and I explained, reasoned and begged. Three out of the four were won over fairly easily. Yet Halim was obstinate. He felt it would be dishonourable for me to do nursing: 'I'd rather be dead than have my sister be seen in the Haifa General Hospital' he protested referring to the main teaching hospital in Palestine. Halim's protest worried me: he was not quite seventeen yet but I knew he could still influence my parents against me. What was I to do? Wadii, my eldest brother came up with a suggestion which actually solved the problem for me. He was working at Lydd – a small town near Jaffa – and happened to be at home on leave at that particular time. He told me that he knew of a good hospital in Jaffa run by the CMS and suggested that he could find out for me whether they trained nurses as well.

The possibility that I might do my training at Jaffa turned out to be acceptable to everybody, including my parents. Even Halim was placated; apparently I could be a nurse as long as it wasn't in Haifa. Wadii was authorised to make enquiries.

In a matter of months I had applied to the Jaffa hospital, visited it and had been accepted there as a student nurse. To my relief, it was very quickly obvious that I had made the right choice. I was in my element; despite the fact that all the teaching was in English, I enjoyed the work. I studied hard and was kept very busy. Above all, I enjoyed the practical side of nursing and liked dealing with the patients. After a period of six months theoretical work, we were introduced to work on the wards.

At the end of the first year, we had to face the examiners and I had to do both theory and practical examinations. All government medical exams were held in Jerusalem and on the bus there I found myself desperately afraid of failing the exams. Sick with worry, I drew close to God for the first time in many months. I asked him to help me during the exams. I argued to myself – and perhaps to him – that I was justified in asking for help: after all, wasn't looking after sick people a form of serving God? True, I acknowledged, I was not serving in China – but surely the location wasn't important? It was the people that mattered. When it came to the exam, I felt that God must have nodded his head in agreement with my rationalization and decided to stand by me. My excitement had died down, my heart had stopped beating wildly, my mind was at peace, I could think clearly and my hand was steady on the paper. All the study and learning I had done in the past months came back to me as I answered both the oral and written questions. After a few weeks, I had my results: I had passed my first year exams. I was delighted.

Being in a CMS hospital, we were encouraged to take part in the Christian work there in our free time and, if appropriate, while on duty. Some staff offered to speak to patients individually, while others took the ward Sunday services. But above all, we were urged to witness to non-Christians and tell them about Christ. It was taken for granted that we would know what to say!

My inadequacy in this area was painfully brought home to me when I found myself caring for an eighteen-year-old Muslim girl, just a few months younger than myself, who was very sick and on the point of death. I tried to make her as comfortable as possible. I so wanted to tell her about God and about Jesus but had no idea what to say or where to begin. In desperation, I urged her to say 'Jesus forgive me and save me.' As I said it, I found myself asking myself what did she – or I, for that matter – know about Jesus, forgiveness or saving? The only response my patient made was to sadly say, 'I don't know how to say "Jesus forgive me and save me"; I can't say "Jesus forgive me and save me"'. Then immediately after that she started repeating the verse from the Koran 'There is only one God and Mohammed is his prophet' until finally she fell silent. I sensed then what I now know as truth: for all my commitment, I had not yet met God as my Saviour. I really did not know him.

Two strange experiences stick in my mind from my days in the CMS hospital in Jaffa. They were strange in the sense that they were beyond any natural explanation but what was perhaps stranger still was the fact that they did not frighten me. Both used to occur at night when I was on duty and both recurred. The first strange experience was the regular appearance of the figure of a man standing in the corridor at the entrance of one of the wards. He was so real that whenever I passed him I would automatically pull the skirt of my uniform against my body so it would not touch him. I always knew when the man was there, even if I had my eyes shut. I never looked into his face; I did not really want to acknowledge his presence and deliberately turned my head and shoulders away from him. He never obstructed my path, spoke to me, or in any way drew attention to himself. He was just there. It was all very real but somehow I was not frightened; it was as if I knew that the stranger had the right to be there. I knew it but I did not want to have anything to do with him.

The second strange experience would also occur on night duty and always happened when I sat down for my snack and cup of coffee. Suddenly from the end of the corridor, where the staircase came up from the ground floor, would appear the figures of three very tiny little girls with bright eyes dressed in sailor suits. They would make their appearance as soon as I sat down to eat: the tops of their heads would show first and then they would emerge and, full of lively energy, would continue on up to the second floor, almost bouncing up the staircase as they went. I was strangely drawn to them but could never see enough of them because as soon as my eye caught theirs they would instantly disappear as if sinking through the tiled floor.

While I was in Jaffa, I came across a number of new inventions. For the first time in my life, I heard the wireless. New electric lights transformed our hospital to daylight at night. Some of our wealthier staff members drove themselves into the hospital grounds in their own automobiles. The technology of the twentieth century was finding its way into Palestine.

I led a busy life. It wasn't just work that kept me busy; there were also many leisure activities. The various social events were however, very different to what I was used to. The CMS hospital was England in miniature and the lifestyle and social customs seemed to be purely English, were untarnished by foreign hands or tongues. So for instance, I was treated to an English Christmas dinner complete with Christmas pudding surrounded by blue flames and twigs of holly carried into the dining room. And at Easter there was turkey stuffed with chestnuts and accompanied by all the trimmings. I enjoyed it all.

Yet life was not all parties and feasting. The life of a nurse involved discipline and there lay a problem: discipline was not one of my natural endowments. It took many years and many tears to acquire an adequate discipline and before I did, my carelessness almost cost me my career. On two or three occasions I was severely reprimanded for being careless and for making mistakes; the latter charge bringing with it a serious danger of dismissal. On one occasion, I was too proud to apologise when I was in the wrong. The Staff Nurse reported me at once to Matron, an English woman, for neglecting to give one of the patients his medication and when I was summoned to see her, her main complaint was that I had not said 'sorry' to the Staff Nurse. I shrugged my shoulders and told her that I had said 'an Arabic sorry'. Mercifully, she did not ask what that was.

After that incident I became convinced that I was being treated unfairly and that I was regularly being given the most unpleasant and uninteresting work on the wards. I made up my mind to leave. Deep down in my heart, I did not want to leave nursing but the problems I was having revived an old concern. I had become certain that missionaries and I could not live together under the same roof. And certainly not for any length of time.

As my second year came to an end I handed in my resignation to Miss Morris, the head of the nursing school. I was anxious to return home in order to consider my situation. I wondered what – if anything – I had accomplished in my life. I felt intensely disillusioned with myself and with the world around me. I sensed that I yearned for something: but what? It eluded me. Even what

I desired seemed to have no consistency: everything seemed stale, empty and pointless.

In the 1920s the political tensions between Arab and Jewish communities in Palestine continued to increase. The Jewish population had not only grown, it had become united and organised and was well represented with the British authorities. In contrast, the Arabs were divided amongst themselves, were often in disarray and were generally ineffectual at getting their case heard with the British. The Jews had an agenda and had vision for the future; we were happy with drifting along. In the summer of 1929, the simmering tension boiled over and rioting flared up again between Jews and Arabs. This time over three hundred were killed and when order was restored, the gap between the two communities was larger than ever.

For me though, the rioting was simply a noisy backdrop against which I wrestled with my own problems. I returned home in Haifa that summer a restless and disillusioned young woman. I was nearly twenty-two and my future was still unclear. I tried to sort out matters in my mind. It was not, I decided, that I wanted to do something different: nursing was the only thing left to me that still had meaning and I was convinced it was one of the few places where my life would not be wasted. But how could I get back to it and complete my training? Who – and where – would accept me now?

Karim, the third brother, had married and his wife, Badia, came to my rescue. In conversation with her, we decided that Haifa General Hospital was probably my only hope and should be my first target. Badia had been a teacher and, when the need arose, could be very charming and persuasive so I left the problem of convincing my parents to her. I applied to the government hospital and was interviewed. Despite an unnecessarily harsh and negative reference for me from the CMS hospital in Jaffa, I was accepted. They either were badly in need of nurses or sensed that Jaffa had been unfair to me.

I studied at Haifa for two years and did well. No one, least of all me, was in doubt about my ability. I tackled the work with great enthusiasm and interest, was always eager to take on new responsibilities and did not show any hesitation to do the mundane tasks that occur in nursing. To no one's surprise, I passed the final exams.

After a week of parties and celebrations at the hospital and at home, I went to the graduation ceremony. In June 1931, I received my nursing certificate from Miss Davis, principal of the nursing school in Haifa. Almost bursting with joy and pride, I untied the red ribbon, unrolled the white paper scroll and read these words:

DEPARTMENT OF HEALTH / GOVERNMENT OF PALESTINE

This is to certify that ***Wadeah Habiby*** *has received in the Government General Hospital at Haifa a course of training in nursing, extending over the full period of 3 years as prescribed by the Government regulations for the training of nurses in Palestine, and that she has successfully completed the necessary examinations. Her name has therefore been entered on the Government register of graduate nurses, in virtue whereof she is entitled to all the rights and privileges of a graduate nurse in Palestine.*

Jerusalem 6th June, 1931
The Director of Health

In July 1931, after a short break, I packed my suitcase to go to Jerusalem for six months training in midwifery. As in Haifa, this government hospital was run mainly by British staff following British standards. I found learning about babies, and delivering and caring for them, very gratifying. I felt I had made the right choice. All my years of struggle and hard work now seemed to be worthwhile. The programme I took required me to do forty deliveries with varying degrees of supervision: including twenty deliveries in hospital and twenty at home. I soon satisfied the requirement and my work was highly recommended. At the end of the training period, I received another diploma.

GOVERNMENT OF PALESTINE/DEPARTMENT OF HEALTH

LICENCE TO PRACTISE THE PROFESSION OF MIDWIFERY

IN PURSUANCE of the powers conferred under the Midwives Ordinance, 1929 authority is given to **WADEAH S HABIBY** *holder of the Certificate of Midwife of the Department of Health, Government of Palestine No 209 to practise the profession of Midwifery within the limits of the jurisdiction and subject to the Laws and Ordinances of the Government of Palestine and to the Regulations and Rules of the Department of Health that may be in force, or may be brought into force, in relation to the practice of Midwifery. IN VIRTUE WHEREOF her name has been entered in the register of Midwives.*

GIVEN UNDER MY HAND THIS 9TH DAY OF FEBRUARY 1932

DIRECTOR DEPARTMENT OF HEALTH

It was at this time that my social life began to change. One of my cousins, Munir began paying me special attention. In those days, it was quite common that a young person would find a marriage partner from within his or her extended family and it wasn't long before there was a general assumption in my family that Munir and I would get married. At the end of my training in Jerusalem, Munir came to Jerusalem in his car, collected me from the gate of the nursing school and drove me home to Haifa.

I was appointed to the Government hospital in Nablus and moved there in March 1932. With eager anticipation and confidence, I saw a new chapter of my life opening before me.

I had no idea how badly my hopes were to be dashed.

CHAPTER 5

Men and Marriage

1932 - 1936

Soon after I settled in at the hospital at Nablus, I was put in charge of the maternity ward. I found being present at the miracle of birth an amazing and humbling experience. Watching babies born, gently ushering them into the world, helping them take their first breath; I loved it all. I could have worked there for ever. It was almost a religious experience; I could imagine my hands as sacred tools in this holiest of tasks. I felt a wave of love for every tiny little face as I bundled it in its blanket and handed it to its mother. There was hardly any time to stop and linger: there always seemed to be more babies waiting. The next step up in my career was to take some home delivery cases. Here the responsibility for every birth was totally mine – if help was needed, I could not turn round and call for it. Yet these home deliveries came and went with great success and I found myself gaining skill and confidence in my work.

The successful delivery of a baby boy always meant presents. I remember how one afternoon at the Nurses Home a large baking tray arrived – it was full of *kenafah,* a sweet of very fine pastry layered with thick fresh cream-like unsalted cheese and drenched with syrup. It was large enough to feed fifty people!

There were two hospitals in Nablus, the Government hospital I was at and, only a short distance away, the CMS mission hospital. Nablus was a Muslim town and being there, I found that I missed the Christian teaching and atmosphere that had surrounded me ever since I was a child. Partly because of that, I became drawn to the regular Christian fellowship meetings at the CMS hospital. I found the Bible teaching there comforting; somehow, it made me feel at home. The messages were clear and direct and I fully agreed with what was said in them. But that was as far as things went and I had no intention of going any further. My youthful passion for missionary work had faded away. God was still far away in heaven: kind, loving and omnipotent, but also distant. In some ways, I was content with that situation. I felt I was doing well in life. 'Thank you very much God, I can manage on my own' was the motto of my life at that time.

Yet beneath the surface, I was not satisfied with my life and I had a deep emptiness in my heart: I hungered for something to fill it. When I probed my unhappiness, I tried to convince myself that the satisfaction my nursing was giving me would soon fill up the gaps and answer my questions. Over my life a small dark cloud of dissatisfaction hovered.

One of the perks of the job was that I did not have far to go when I needed medical attention; my first ever experience of being a patient in a hospital came as a result of an attack of appendicitis. Being a nurse there, I was given first class treatment, but I also witnessed the jealousy and wrangling between doctors. I was Dr. H's patient, but Doctor M. just went ahead and did the operation himself. It was something of an eye-opener.

Despite being some way from my family, I stayed in close contact with them. Munir regularly visited me and eventually, to what appeared to be general approval, he and I became engaged to be married. I was fond of Munir but not in love with him; but I was 25 – 'getting on' for an unmarried woman and there were pressures to get married. Munir had moved to Jaffa where he worked and with his car found it no hardship to get to Nablus, a mere forty minutes drive away. I got to see a great deal of him and also his sister who kept house for him.

Occasionally, Munir's brother Shafiq would come for weekends too and as a threesome we would go together to parties, dancing, cinemas and for meals. Cousin Shafiq was a wonderful dancing partner – together we perfected the Charleston, Foxtrot and Quickstep and many others. Life was good, there was so much fun and enjoyment to be had and, on the surface at least, my life seemed to lack nothing. The days of toeing the line dictated by father, brothers and society were long gone. I was young, strong and independent; I was a social success. Whatever I wanted I simply reached out for. I did not wait for fashion to come to me, I was ahead of fashion – I was ahead of life. Wherever there was anything new, Wadeah was there first. Yet every so often, my satisfaction in my work and my social success would be broken by strange yearnings for something else.

Soon my wedding day loomed and I gave my notice in to the hospital at Nablus. Munir and I prepared to start married life together. Very soon though, I realised that there were issues with Munir that I needed to think about. The first issue was relatively minor: Munir had somewhat insulted my parents by not going to see them first (as custom demanded) and asking if he might be engaged to me. For all my ideas of being a free and independent woman, I still valued good manners. Far from being daring and exciting, Munir's action had troubled me; it seemed to show that he did not value conformity and respectability. The second issue was that, quite simply, I was not sure I wanted to be married to Munir. Once the excitement of the engagement had subsided and turned into weeks of getting to know each other and planning for our future, it had become clear to me that, once married, I would simply become Munir's wife and no more. I would have to accept all his decisions and to follow where he led. The idea frightened me: I could not imagine the strange creature that I would have to turn into. I would lose all that I had achieved so far in becoming who I was now. My mother was fifteen years younger than my father but she had never lost her identity and was always a strong factor in our family. I could settle for nothing less than she had. Pondering these two issues, I suddenly knew for certain that Munir was not really for me and that I could never be happy with him.

I broke off our engagement. I gave him back his ring, said goodbye to my friends and colleagues at the hospital in Nablus – it was too late to take back my notice – and returned home to my parents in Haifa. I had not been enough in love with Munir to be broken-hearted; nevertheless, I felt a deep void in my life. These feelings were partly due to the failure of my relationship with Munir but also because the old emptiness had returned. Now though, I no longer had my work to hide my need of something more in my life.

After living and working out in the world on my own, returning to my parent's house was very difficult. Although my father and mother were more than glad to see me, I felt like I was trying to fit myself into the make believe world of a doll's house. I had changed and home had changed. My three older brothers were already married. Two of the younger ones, Halim and Nakhleh, were now working and doing well enough for themselves that they could help out financially at home. The two youngest brothers and my sister were also growing up; doing well at school and able to look after themselves.

Strangely, I found that now I had come home, I could, for the first time, see that my mother was a woman in her own right, and not just a wife and a mother. My mother was as proud of me as though she had discovered a new daughter. She now treated me as a friend and an equal rather than a daughter and I detected respect in her eyes for me. I was relieved to find that she was not upset at the news that I had broken off my engagement to my cousin. It emerged that, on the contrary, she and my father were relieved. They had never really liked cousin Munir and that dislike was mutual. My uncle's family and ours were not on good terms.

It was at this time, barely noted by us, that an event took place which, fifteen years later was to seal the fate of

Palestine. Alarmed by the riots of 1929, the British had begun to restrict Jewish immigration to Palestine in the hope of ending the tensions between the Arabs and the Jews. It was a policy that might have worked except, that in 1933 Adolf Hitler came to power in Germany. Worried by his Anti-Semitic agenda, many Jews began to leave Germany and turned their eyes towards Palestine. Hitherto Jewish emigration to Palestine had been driven by the pull of the ideal of a Jewish homeland. Now with the rise of fascism, there was a push as well. Jewish immigration began to increase again.

In Haifa, I found out that the news that I had broken off my engagement had spread fast. I had not long returned home when, one morning my mother came to my room, holding her head high and with a twinkle in her eye. I sensed she was the bearer of important news and what it was soon emerged. A young man was asking for my hand in marriage. His two sisters, R. and N. had visited my parents and asked if they could bring their brother on their next visit. The two sisters were from the Musallams, a good family of reputable social standing in our community; the sisters were certainly well educated, speaking English and German fluently. In due course, I met their brother Khalil and found him rather quiet but nice. Due to continuous ill health he had not completed his schooling and did not have his sisters' educational attainments; nevertheless he had a profession – he was a shoemaker.

Pressure to accept came from my parents. I was almost twenty-seven and a girl of such an age, still living at her parents' house could only be waiting for one thing – a good husband and marriage. A second visit by the two sisters – with their brother this time – concluded the matter. I found myself saying 'yes'. It was a very strange 'yes' – cold and impersonal. Yet I felt I had to accept; most of my friends were either already married or getting married.

It was, of course, a foolish decision. I had been 'a woman of the world'; I was fashionable, I loved music, I had danced the latest steps, I enjoyed the good things in this life, I had been a success in a demanding job, I could look after myself socially and financially: yet I decided to marry Khalil.

Why did I do it? All I can think is deep down in me, beneath the new found sophistication and confidence, there still existed that shy and quiet little village girl from Shafa 'Amr. And it was that simple trusting girl, the one who in the field at sunset had offered herself a sacrifice to God if he would stop the war, who said 'yes' to this most unequal of marriages.

We were married one cold Saturday in December 1934. My dress was white, the flowers were beautiful and orange blossom filled St. Luke's Church in Haifa with incense like perfume. It was a cold winter's day, the church was crowded with well-wishers, family and friends, but outside the sky was thick with dark clouds and rain. I saw the smiles and heard the congratulations; my heart trembled at the thunder and shivered at the cold of the unknown future.

Our honeymoon was deferred till a later date – springtime perhaps – so we could first arrange somewhere to live and apply for passports. Neither Khalil nor I had been outside Palestine and the plan was for us to go to Egypt for our honeymoon. Khalil had a half sister who lived in Cairo with her husband and family. It was decided that in the meantime our temporary home was to be in Nazareth where the Musallams had a large family house that was used mainly during summer holidays by various family members.

I quickly began to realise that I was expected to fit in. My father-in-law made it obvious that I was expected to supplement our family income. In fact, it was soon apparent that they saw me as the main breadwinner. "Where would you like to hang your 'midwife' sign," he said to me one day soon after we arrived in Nazareth.

In a blinding fury, I only saw strange people trying to organize *my* life; wanting to change me and mould me into a stranger that I no longer recognized. Someone else might have given in and bowed their head submissively but it wasn't me. Part of my headstrong, independent spirit was that such pressures never worked; they just made me more rebellious rather than subdued.

As things worked out, we did not stay long in Nazareth. Being a newcomer to the area myself, I was not able to establish my midwifery work. The house too, turned out to be a problem as in the summer other members of the family arrived and expected to use it. These included Khalil's sister who came from Egypt with her large family as well as his two unmarried sisters R. and N. who normally lived and worked in Haifa.

So before the holiday overcrowding began, Khalil and I returned to Haifa and rented a small apartment in a house that belonged to one of my brothers. There Khalil opened a cobbler's shop but found little work. I also started working as a midwife and a district nurse, having applied for – and received my licence – to practice home deliveries. Soon I had a small list of expectant mothers in my diary to be attended to: there were antenatal visits, delivery and then postnatal care.

Soon I too was pregnant and earning an income became vital in order to support both of us and the baby that was on the way. Khalil found himself under continuous strain and pressure. We were surrounded by many members of the Habiby family, many of whom were successful in their businesses and jobs. Honour demanded that he be seen to be doing well in his work. In moving from Nazareth to Haifa our roles had been reversed; he was now in the uncomfortable situation of being the stranger in unfamiliar territory. My own attitude could not have helped matters for me either as unwittingly, I found myself comparing my husband negatively to my brothers who were very quickly shaking off their humble beginnings and becoming successful in a fast changing society. They had businesses that were well established, owned their own houses, had flats for rented accommodation, and had families that were growing in number and prosperity.

A further problem for Khalil was the fact that, quite simply, I was not the wife he had expected. He had wanted someone to pamper him on demand, to provide him with his every little need and treat him like an invalid. I would do none of these things. Under these pressures my husband turned more and more to his family, particularly to his two unmarried full sisters who lived in Haifa. They had always had a close relationship; they had cared for him when he was still only a child after their mother had died and continued to love him dearly. Although their father's second marriage produced other children - three sisters and two brothers – Khalil remained the special responsibility of Radia. and Naeema. Never a strong or healthy child, his many ailments meant that his schooling and education suffered accordingly and he had had to rely on his sisters a great deal. Now, as in the past, he turned to them for advice, comfort and support. They were generous and well-meaning, but they became the third party in my marriage. Given that our married life was already unbalanced, their involvement made things dangerously unstable.

I began to resent Khalil's sisters. Coming home in the evening at the end of a working day I would find myself faced with money gifts earmarked for an 'extra nourishing diet' for our brother. Their well-meaning advice was also intrusive; Khalil would tell me that 'my sister thinks I should not be working so hard'. I began to find their many other questions and unasked for advice all far too much.

Worst of all, I began to despise Khalil. A strong willed and caring husband would have led me like a sheep, but Khalil was neither. I realised bitterly that for me there was nothing in this man that I either loved, cared for, or even needed.

I was now utterly disillusioned with life. Before marriage I could please myself aware that the only person to suffer was myself – now by my actions I was ruining two people, my husband and myself. I could see how the mistakes I made were resulting in misery, heartache and shame. The situation seemed doomed. I knew I could not change my husband, and I had no idea that I could change. The only question I had was how to get out of the impasse.

Our baby, a daughter, was born in March 1936 and we named her Siham. For the next forty days our lives were like the breaking of sea waves on the rocks – no sooner was the froth from one row settled when the next row would shake the foundations. Radia and Naeema did not help; particularly offensive to me – as a trained midwife – was their concern for the baby. I found myself facing questions such as: 'Is she sleeping on her tummy or her back, all or part of the time?'

Finally, Khalil decided that we had to leave our flat and move to another place. That was my cue. He could move wherever he wanted, but I wasn't going anywhere. I told him that the baby and I were staying where we were. The determination in my voice and attitude left him with no room for discussion or argument. Khalil left the next day. A strange calm descended on our home; never in all our short married life had it known such peace and quiet. Yet it was a curiously evasive peace. It seemed to cling to the walls round the flat, to merge with the air in the house and to surround my little baby daughter yet it eluded me. This peace was a stranger to me.

I became bitter. Where was the peace and contentment I had been pursuing all my life? Peace, I knew existed but all I could find was emptiness.

However, hand in hand with my stubbornness went determination. And here, thrown down to the bottom, I resolved that I was not giving up. I might have separated from my husband but I was certainly not defeated. I was free and I had a most precious possession – my daughter. For her sake, I was determined to struggle and win back the life I had lost. I determined that I would fight to reclaim the lost joy and bury the tears. I would do it for my daughter, and I would do it my way without the help of others, whether they were God or man.

Oh foolish heart, how slow to learn. Not content with almost ruining my life, my own stubbornness was now putting me on a course that threatened to destroy the dearest being to me on earth, my own daughter.

CHAPTER 6

Separation

My family, as close knit as ever, rallied round and offered me any assistance that I needed. My mother began to look after Siham so that I was able to return to work, delivering other women's babies. Yet although my family supported me, they were unhappy at the turn of events. They were decidedly against the separation; socially it was still considered taboo to have a marriage break down and any divorce would be embarrassing for the whole family. My younger brother Halim, who had been against the marriage in the first place, was furious with me for allowing the relationship to deteriorate so badly; he expected me to make it up with Khalil and to return to him as soon as possible. His arguments fell on deaf ears. My newfound freedom was pleasant to me and I was in no mood to be persuaded to give it up, either now or in the future. I had, I insisted, every right to a normal happy life. Halim and the rest of the family could do and say what they pleased but I was not returning to my husband and the arguments, fighting and beatings.

So, with the help of my family, my life returned to some sort of stability. I maintained my prized independence by renting a small flat on the lower slopes of Mount Carmel off Abbas Street. The arrangement where my mother looked after Siham worked out very satisfactorily. My private maternity cases kept me busy and brought in a reasonable income for the daily needs of my daughter and myself. I had my independence and freedom but I found I didn't want to socialize or mix with other people – especially men – who I had suddenly decided that I hated. I had been hurt, and as those who are hurt do, I had created barriers to prevent it happening again.

Such leisure time as I had was for my daughter and her alone. I found Siham an extraordinary consolation at this time. Her tiny sweet face, full of peace and trust, was like a candle shedding light into the shattered darkness of my life. Whether sleeping or waking, she seemed able to soothe my troubled spirit. Siham did not develop the common baby habit of sucking her finger, but instead, whether in her cot or her pram, she would stretch out her arm to me and I had to hold her little hand in mine until sleep or contentment came over her. The trust and peace my daughter had when she held my hand only seemed to highlight my own lack of any such security.

I became bored and sought an antidote for my boredom in reading. I read anything and everything and even read the Bible but I neither understood nor cared about what I read there. At that time, religion was of no importance to me, but was simply something, along with other social activities, that I did for the sake of my family and the community around me. My daughter's christening was typical. We had arranged it as a private affair with only a few chosen invitees for the afternoon of Sunday, 5th September 1936. My husband was not even informed of the event, let alone invited. Word must have reached him however because he was seen pacing up and down outside the church but no one asked him in to attend his daughter's ceremony. The Reverend

Yusuf Fleihan officiated at the service and Siham's godmothers were my cousin Violet and my sister-in-law, Latifeh. My own attitude was, I'm afraid, that it was just a charade that I had to act in. It was an empty ceremony, a social occasion, and nothing more than that.

The weeks lengthened into months and my pattern of work and pleasure became more established. On the surface, I remained carefree and my efforts to push away the troubled emptiness that existed deep down in my life were largely successful. Occasionally though, the cheerful sunshine of my life was blotted out by black clouds of worry. And sometimes there were crises. At twelve months, Siham developed German Measles, which was taking its normal course until one night when she had a sudden rise in her fever and went into convulsions. As a nurse, I should have been able to deal with the situation but instead I panicked. I ran across the yard to mother's house just ten metres away; she was at home, came over immediately and called the doctor. Fearful for the life of my dear daughter, I turned once more to God, that old acquaintance whose existence I had so long forgotten. With a heart rending 'Please don't let her die! Don't take her away from me, she's all I've got' I called on God to save my baby.

God heard my cry and, in his mercy, answered it: the crisis passed and Siham recovered. I shudder to think of the consequences if he had not answered that prayer. Had my daughter been taken from me, I fear I would never have turned back to God and my soul would have been lost eternally.

Yet the old pattern now repeated itself. With Siham safe, I forgot about God. Once more, he was left outside my life.

The months passed. In the background, the problems of Palestine mounted and the storm clouds grew ever darker. Jewish immigration continued, given a new energy by events in Hitler's Germany. In 1935, alone, nearly 62,000 Jews entered Palestine and Arabs began to realise that, if immigration continued, they would soon be in the minority. By now, both Jews and Arabs had acquired weapons and were developing militias. In 1936, events took a new and ugly turn with widespread armed conflict between the two communities. The British found themselves attacked by both sides and over thirty members of the British Army were killed. The British response was a Royal Commission, which in 1937 decided that the gulf between the two communities, was so great that Palestine would have to be divided between Jews and Arabs. It was a proposal that pleased no one. The Royal Commission was followed by reports, conferences and in 1939, a White Paper which was sympathetic to the Arabs.

These local efforts to make peace were all undermined by global events, when the long impending European war erupted in September 1939. In some ways, the Second World War had little impact on Palestine. Palestine itself held no real strategic value to either side in the Second World War, except inasmuch as it guarded the eastern side of the vital Suez Canal link to the Indian Ocean. In the early days of the war as the Germans and the Italians moved towards Cairo, there was some concern that Palestine would fall but that worry was removed by the battle of El Alamein. Unlike the First World War, there was to be no land fighting in Palestine. Yet in other ways, the Second World War was to be disastrous for Palestine as it set the stage for the catastrophe of 1948.

For the first year or so, the Second World War seemed very distant to us although we followed its progress. We were far more concerned about the internal situation in Palestine. Most Jewish immigrants entered Palestine through the port of Haifa and it was impossible to conceal their numbers. And partly in response, there were also an increasing number of armed Palestinians quite openly patrolling the streets as a self-appointed 'Home Guard'. Yet heedless of the global war or the dark clouds looming over the future of Palestine, my life continued much as before. Then in late 1940, things started to change.

It was now almost four years since I left my husband. I found myself increasingly busy with my work; I had become well known and accepted as a midwife and my workload had increased. Yet I was seeing less and less of Siham, who was now an active and headstrong four-year old. Nevertheless, I confidently presumed that she was being well looked after by my mother and other relatives while I was out at work. That I presumed too much was demonstrated when one day, returning home after a case visit, I found my daughter going through one of her tantrums. When I spoke to her, I was horrified to find that she hurled every swear word I had ever heard at me. Shocked, I wondered how she had picked up this appalling vocabulary. The answer turned out to be that the municipality was doing some road repairs almost under our windows and my daughter had found it amusing to watch the men at work and listen to their conversation. I took it as a warning that I could not just assume that my daughter would be alright; I had to do something.

The most obvious answer was to send Siham to school, but nursery schools were not common in those days and few schools would take a four-year-old. The English High School, a private and church-based school, was the nearest to us, but they only took pupils who were five. Still, I had to try. The next day, having made an appointment, I went to see Miss Emery, the headmistress. Miss Emery was an austere English woman with penetrating blue eyes. It was immediately obvious that she had done her homework and knew exactly who I was and what my home situation was. Having anticipated the sort of objections, Miss Emery would raise, I had prepared my answers accordingly and, I thought, satisfactorily. My confidence was shattered when she played her trump card: 'You do realize that Miss Musallam is our kindergarten teacher and your daughter will be taught by her. You have no objections I presume?' Radia Musallam was my sister-in-law and my sworn enemy. The headmistress must have been fully aware of this from the local community gossip. Caught on the horns of a dilemma, I hesitated for a few seconds before giving my careful reply: 'Miss Musallam is an excellent and well-known infant teacher, I have no qualms whatsoever about my daughter being taught by her.'

In fact, the first part of my answer was true: Miss Musallam's fame as a kindergarten teacher had spread far and wide in Palestine. Many a parent could be heard proudly saying their son or daughter had their first two years of schooling at the hands of Miss Musallam. If Miss Musallam had laid the foundations in a child's life, it seemed to be assumed that they were well on the road for a distinguished social and academic life. My qualms lay in two areas; having to deal with my sister-in-law and paying the high fees that such a school demanded. Yet my sister-in-law proved more amicable than I had expected and soon announced how proud she was to have her bright and lively four-year-old niece in her educational care. Siham was, she proclaimed, a Musallam through and through.

I had heard little about Khalil for some time and had assumed that he was in Nazareth but at this time his family started to be restive again. Through mutual acquaintances, they let it be known that they expected me to give Khalil a divorce since I was neither planning to return to him, nor intending to heal the breach with him. I soon discovered out the reason for their request: they were already arranging another marriage for him. On principle – or perhaps just to annoy them – I refused to agree to their demands: in fact, the matter made me all the more intent to carry on life as I was.

Shortly after this, I found out that Khalil had not returned to Nazareth at all but was still living in Haifa. There, apparently all but forgotten even by his beloved sisters, he lived alone in a small apartment above his workshop.

This news about Khalil had a strange effect on me. I felt a sudden surge of sympathy and pity for the man whom I had known so briefly but whom I was now so far apart from. It was a feeling that I did not quash and as I considered Khalil and his plight, I found myself engulfed by a raging sea of conflicting emotions. I had a strong yearning to help and comfort this lonely man, to make a home for him and for us to share our life together in total harmony. Then, as a reaction, the searing scenes from those painful days would rush back into my memory with a jolt and I would remind myself that it would be the same Khalil: the man would not have changed.

Although it never occurred to me to ask whether *I* personally could change, the matter of Khalil raised the issue of change. Could someone change dramatically? Could someone who was hated become someone who was loved or, if not loved, at least cared for and embraced? What, if any, power could engineer such a change? And if such a transformation could occur, then what was its price?

Without realising it, I had reached the crossroads in my life.

CHAPTER 7

Conversion

Could someone change dramatically? It was a question whose answer was, quite literally, to be on my doorstep.

Munir, my cousin and my ex-fiancé, had just moved back to Haifa and one day he came to visit me with Khazneh, his wife. I was struck immediately by his appearance: my jolly and very worldly cousin now seemed a very different person. There was a serene shine to his face and eyes that seemed more than even a happy marriage could bring. He and Kazneh seemed dying to tell me something, as if they had a secret to share with me.

I had half assumed that they were expecting a baby but that was not their secret: sadly, they were still childless. It was something else. All of a sudden, the words tumbled out; some from him, some from her: some familiar, others incomprehensible. 'We've become Christians, true Christians' they both said at once. '"Jesus died for us, He has saved us from our sins; we love Him. We know God as we've never known him before. He walks and lives with us – He's real, He's alive. He has *changed* our lives!'.

As I listened in astonishment, they explained what had happened. There had been strange happenings in Amman, Jordan where in 1933 the amazing visions of a woman, Umm Saleem Kaawar, had challenged the churches. This had lead to a work of the Holy Spirit in which those who were just nominal Christians, or even not Christians at all, had come to know Jesus Christ and his power and had an experience of a God who was alive. God's Spirit had touched the lives of

Munir and Khazneh, changing them and they were now full of joy and eager to serve God in whatever way he wanted.

I found Munir and Khazneh's account and their enthusiasm almost overwhelming. Yet one thing was both clear and intriguing: these two had changed. I had been wondering about the possibility of change: they had experienced it. Before Munir and Khazneh left, they invited me to attend one of their meetings at Bethesda Hall, a place where a Christian group, the Brethren, met. Out of curiosity, I went to the meeting where I sat through the singing and the sermon, which were all in English. I found nothing there that remotely touched my heart, let alone changed my life and I could hardly wait for the end of the service. When the service finished, I got up from my seat and left immediately without talking to anyone. The barriers that I had put up in my life to protect me from further hurt were not going to be so easily overcome. Despite this, Munir and Khazneh were not put off but instead continued to show kindness to me, introducing me to their friends and opening their home to me. They did not pressurise me concerning Christian matters but I was to find out later that they constantly prayed for me.[1]

Shortly after this, Munir and his friends began to get very excited about the visit of the Reverend Roy Whitman to Palestine. Roy, it turned out, was a young Canadian minister who had settled in Amman, Jordan with his English wife.[2] He had been there during the 'Umm Saleem' visions and had written down all the happenings, which were later published in a small booklet called 'Signs and Wonders in Rabbaih, Ammon.' Roy Whitman had been invited to talk at various churches in Palestine with the hope of encouraging a spiritual reawakening among Christians, as well as reaching out to those of other faiths with the good news of Jesus.

---

[1] Among the members of Bethesda Assembly Hall then were a Mr. and Mrs. Young from England: many years later I was to meet their son Bill and his wife Rosemary in Bedford.

[2] Roy was to have an extraordinary ministry in Jordan that lasted for sixty years, ending only with his death.

Cousin Munir suggested inviting Roy Whitman for a series of meetings at Bethesda Hall. The elders there however refused, so he approached St. John's Anglican Church with his proposal. Contrary to all expectations, they welcomed the idea and the meetings went ahead. Many people were invited for the meetings and hundreds turned up.

One evening, I went along to see what the fuss was all about. An extraordinary thing happened: as the preacher started to speak, he seemed to be transformed in my eyes so that it was Jesus himself who was standing up in the pulpit, explaining and pleading. I had no idea what was being said and from where in the Bible the message came. All I knew was that I was meeting Jesus Christ for the first time in my life and my soul went out to him. The meeting came to an end and the preacher invited those who would like to make a commitment to accept God in their lives to stand up and then stay behind to have a word with him. I stood up along with many others and stayed behind, but when I saw the Reverend Whitman later talking to others my immediate reaction was to get out of the church. I now saw only an ordinary man and I had nothing to say to him. The image of Jesus that I saw in him earlier in the evening was gone. Before he had a chance to speak to me, I turned round and left the church.

I returned on the second and third evenings, (when one of my brothers Adib, was there too) but each time, I left without asking questions or receiving enlightenment. I felt drawn to these meetings as if by a strange power and looked forward to each one with an overwhelming sense of deep joy. Eventually the meetings came to an end and my life returned to its normal routine. Yet it was not quite business as usual; something somewhere had changed.

Within a few months Roy Whitman was offered – and accepted – a second invitation to speak in our church. As before, the church was full every evening and, as before, I went along. Yet this time as I saw the preacher, there was rebellion in my heart. For some reason, he did not preach from the pulpit. I thought that he looked insignificant and rather silly and found that I could not take his words seriously. I wondered why I still came to hear him. The last evening though, was different. He simply started by closing his eyes and praying silently, then opening his Bible, he read the following words: 'Peace I leave with you, my Peace I give to you; not as the world gives do I give to you. Let not your hearts be troubled neither let them be afraid.'[3] His voice was not particularly loud but his words seemed to reverberate and echo and re-echo inside me as if hammering in through my ears and into my heart. I could not escape the persistent pressure of that voice. Suddenly, the speaker had vanished and, once more, Jesus was there before me. I realised that he was offering me the peace that I was seeking and that I did not even know existed. I saw that I had wanted a peace that the world should have given me by right, but didn't. Yet this Jesus was offering me something infinitely better; a personal peace with the power to remove fear and anxiety. Those words of Jesus lifted and carried me far above my circumstances; I found myself wondering if this was a taste of what this power could accomplish in my life? My heart was overflowing with joy, peace and love. Yet I knew that what had happened was more than just an emotional effect: I knew I was utterly transformed. This time I did not need to wait behind at the end of the meeting to talk to anyone. I knew, without a shadow of a doubt, what I wanted to do. I wanted to get home as quickly as possible, open my Bible and read those words again – those and many more.

It was not long before Roy Whitman made his third visit to Haifa. This actually brought him to my parents' house. A meeting had been arranged at the Habiby family home and was held in the large lounge. Family members, neighbours and new converts were all assembled to hear this by now

---

[3] John 14.27

well-known preacher. Mrs Whitman was there too and sang, for the first time, an Arabic hymn written for her with the Arabic title 'Separate me from the crowds and draw me to you, Lord Jesus.' Mrs Whitman had an extraordinary, almost hypnotic voice which compelled people to listen to the message of the song. After her husband spoke, some people stood up and told how God had saved them from their sins, enabled them to overcome addictions to drink, gambling and other evils. Others prayed openly, committing their lives to God.

And Wadeah Habiby? Well, pleasant as it would be to say that everything was now plain sailing for me, it would not be true. All I knew at that stage was that I had come to follow Jesus and was beginning to learn from him in the school of life. Reading the Bible had become a source of great help, joy and encouragement to me. There was something new in my life and that it was very good; I wanted to tell the whole world 'to taste and see that the Lord is good'[4].

I had still not really understood that the true Christian life was a new and radical beginning. I was still reluctant to see the word 'conversion' as applying to me. I insisted to myself that it was all very well for thieves, drunks, addicts and criminals to be 'converted', but did such a word really apply to respectable church folk? In the end an acquaintance asked me 'Is it true that you are really converted?' A verse in the Bible I had read earlier, flashed into my memory: 'Whoever acknowledges me before men I will acknowledge him before my father in Heaven. But whoever disowns me before men, I will disown him before my father in Heaven'[5]. I realised that the exact name that people gave this experience of knowing Christ was irrelevant at that moment; the real issue was whether I would admit knowing him or not, in front of this person. I knew I had to give a positive answer: 'Yes I am,' I admitted, without shame or embarrassment.

[4] Psalm 34.8
[5] Matthew 10.32-33

As the news of my conversion spread around among my friends and acquaintances, people automatically expected me to return to my husband. They took it for granted it was the 'Christian' thing to do. Bishop McKinness had a talk with me and tried to convince me to return to Khalil as did Najib Kub'ain, the new minister at St. John's. Fareedeh Taweel, a nursing colleague and a member of the Haifa Brethren group spoke to me as a 'sister in Christ' and told me that a rebellious spirit was from the devil and, that as a Christian, I should be obedient to God's word. My initial response was to reject every word of advice that related to my marriage. The demands of a Christian life were very important to me and I was aware of them, but I could not handle the pressures from people trying to influence my decision and I turned away from them. One evening at home, I prayed to God and tried to make a deal with him: 'I'll put my daughter in a boarding school, get myself a car and go round and tell people about God's love and forgiveness and witness to them. I'll do all this, go abroad to foreign countries – even to China, Lord, but don't ask me to return to my husband.'

At this time, I found that the presence of Jesus in my life was very much like that mysterious figure I used to see when on night duty in the hospital wards; the man who never said a word but who just stood there with head inclined to one side, silent and waiting. He had never made a demand, but I had always avoided looking into his face. I turned to Jesus and asked what he wanted me to do. His name, 'Man of Sorrows,'[6] gave me the answer. 'Would I return to my husband?' he seemed to ask. It was a painful demand and one that was very much against my wishes. I hesitated. My memory took me back to a vivid dream I had the time just before my daughter was born in which I was presented with a vase which had a single rose, only to find that it was replaced by another which contained three roses. Did the

[6] Isaiah 53.3

dream imply I would return to my husband and have more children?

I found that mentally, I had now accepted all the arguments that I should return to Khalil but emotionally my struggle was just beginning. I turned to God in prayer asking him to change my heart and enable me to take this step. Munir and a few Christians I met at his house, also encouraged me, particularly concerning the practicalities of any reconciliation procedure; praying with me and for me. Oddly, enough my family, especially my brother Halim, did not want to have anything to do with this new development; they were certain that I would be making an even greater mistake than before. I had lost the sympathy of those friends who originally tried to bring about a reconciliation between Khalil and me.

So now what could I do? I trusted God and I had the unshakeable feeling of the Lord leading me by the hand just as you would a small child, gently and reassuringly saying 'we'll work something out.'

God did just that. That year, 1940, the Regional Anglican community ministers had their annual conference in Haifa. I went to the final session, which was open to all church members. My heart was expectant, but wary of new developments, not knowing how, or when, God would choose to execute his will. I was very conscious that he was with me constantly and at times, even one or two steps ahead of me. Yet I was cautious and even fearful. That evening, as I sat in one of the pews, my heart started pounding as I saw, right in front of me, my two sisters-in-law. Their presence didn't make matters any easier and in order to avoid meeting them, I made up my mind to leave just before the end. During the last hymn, I made my way out but only to be greeted at the door by an acquaintance who said that the Reverend Kub'ain, the minister of the Jerusalem church, wanted to see me. Would I wait for him? I waited outside in the car park as the rest of the congregation came out. I was alone; I knew the struggle was over and I felt that my own will had been hammered into a pulp. Bitter tears streamed down my face. I went back in through a side entrance and saw the minister waiting inside the vestry. He seemed to sense that the decision was made and said to me, 'God will give you the strength to return to your husband and will answer your prayers.' Arrangements were made and the following Saturday, the Reverend Kub'ain arrived at my parents' house accompanied by a couple of friends and my husband, and the reconciliation took place there between us.

It was a month before we actually set up home together again. The flat I had was too small for the three of us so we waited until we found a larger apartment that had become available at the building of my eldest brother, Wadii. Khalil and I moved in and restarted our life together, trying to put the broken pieces back into a meaningful relationship.

CHAPTER 8

Family and New Experiences

I was not at all sure what to expect in my new life back with Khalil. Had the separation affected him? And, if so, in what ways? And in my life, there was a totally new factor: God. How was he going to affect things? It was no longer Khalil versus me, there was God as well. Would this new influence make our life together run more smoothly than before, or would it heighten our differences? How would I react to any confrontation or disagreement? Could the Lord make me more malleable and cool down my quick flaring temper so that I could accept Khalil and his failings? *That* surely was going to take a lifetime to accomplish. I was well aware of the devil's power and was sure that, having taken a stand as a Christian, he would try his utmost to discourage me with failure at every turn and junction of life's way.

Such challenges made me depend all the more on God for help. I found myself praying hard concerning the many questions and decisions that I faced. To my amazement, I found the answers were always in God's word. One such instance of this came up in connection with my brother Emile when he declared himself an atheist. At about the same time as I became a true Christian, Emile had been searching genuinely for 'the truth'. He had spent three consecutive days roaming alone on Mount Carmel near our home with a spiritual battle raging in his heart. He had cried out and called on whatever God or power there was, to answer him and 'to send his spirit on him as he did on Moses, Jesus and Mohammed.' There, sadly, the battle was lost; I am certain that had he sought God through Jesus, the Saviour on the cross, things might have been different. Emile came back home after his 'mountain experience', deflated, hurt and blaspheming God's name. My Christian life was still at an early stage; as Emile kept swearing and denying God's existence my unhelpful response was to throw my slipper at his face. My failure to help my brother saddened me and as I prayed and read God's word, I realised that kindness, gentleness and love were the best means of drawing people to Christ.

One lesson I had to learn very soon after returning to my husband concerned children. I was determined not to have any more: one daughter was enough. The main reason for my objection to further children was financial: I felt we needed the extra income, which meant that I had to continue with my work. Siham was already at an expensive private school and she lacked nothing: toys, clothes, books were in plentiful supply and were always the best. Besides, we had enjoyed travelling and holidaying together and I was not prepared to let go of these things. So I felt that all common sense and wisdom pointed to us having no more children. God however reminded me that my husband had a point of view too and I felt that he asked me if I would say 'No' if Khalil wished to have more children. He did wish just that: I didn't say no and eventually we did have more children. Thinking of this in my eighty-ninth year, I look back to that particular lesson and give thanks to God for his good guidance in this matter: How I thank God with all my heart for the blessing of our children!

Siham, now almost five was very excited at having a 'father' at home and went round her cousins and friends telling everyone 'the father' is here. Yet for me, my fresh start with my husband and daughter had no magical qualities. Indeed, for me, the old familiar emptiness began slowly spreading its tentacles around me, binding and imprisoning me. Much, if not all of the problem was spiritual; despite my eagerness to progress in the Christian life, I had entered a period of cooling interest and growing indifference and had even begun to neglect the reading of the Bible. I could find little joy in meeting and being with other Christians. Before too long, my life seemed as if a hot dry dusty wind was sweeping through it and I found myself once more thirsting for something new, unknown and unattainable.

One night, a dream shook me out of my apathy and despair. In my dream, I saw some young women sitting by the edge of a pool, their shiny golden hair cascading over their shoulders and down their backs. Then, as I looked on in amazement, their beautiful hair suddenly changed to an ugly grey wiry mass. Before I could cry out in horror, the young women, who had seen what had happened to them reflected in the water, bent over until their hair dipped into the water. Two or three times, they bowed their heads slowly to meet the sparkling ripples as they submerged their hair which, as it finally came out of the water, was totally restored to its original glory and beauty. The dream did not fade away and the following day, as I puzzled over the meaning of some verses from Ephesians '...with the washing of water by the word'[7] that I had read earlier without understanding, it now became perfectly clear. God had taught me a new lesson about growing in holiness through reading his word and I returned to reading the Bible.

For all my failings, I did make some progress as a Christian and my ears slowly became more receptive to God's Word and his guidance in my life. Gradually, my independent and headstrong nature began to learn the meaning of submission and following the path of obedience. Some verses in Isaiah became very relevant to me: '...He wakens my ear to hear as those who are taught. The Lord God has opened my ears and I was not rebellious.[8] God's word was educating me; when I obeyed, I knew contentment and when I resisted, I lost all peace.

---

[7]Ephesians 5.26
[8]Isaiah 50.4-5

Outside, the effects of the war were becoming more and more prominent. By July 1941, many food items had become rationed, and such items that weren't rationed, weren't available. Suddenly, even trivial items of food became important. I remember Siham's 'egg bag', a small orange cloth bag that she would take to school every Wednesday morning. There each child was given three eggs for the week to take home. 'Mummy,' Siham told me, the first time she brought her 'booty' home, 'the teacher said these eggs were for us children, not for our parents.' Miraculously, her eggs survived the journey.

Palestine was not only affected by the shortage of food in those days, but also by air raids which were an increasingly regular occurrence. Haifa was the terminus of the oil pipeline from Iraq and the site of a huge oil refinery which supplied the needs of the Allied forces in Palestine and elsewhere. The refinery became the target of German bombers and by summer 1941 we seemed to be spending more time in the sticky and sweaty air raid shelters. As Khalil had started working in the oil refinery, I now had a new set of fears to concern me.

As if the air raids and rationing weren't enough, the tensions between the Jews and the Arabs had risen to new levels. Even during peacetime, the British had found policing Palestine hard and now, preoccupied by waging war against Germany, they found it almost impossible. Indeed, the Arabs felt that they had ceased to bother. Illegal Jewish immigration continued and more and more land was sold, often unlawfully, to Jewish buyers. There were all too believable rumours of Jewish atrocities against Arabs and fear and uncertainty undermined the stability of the country. The effects of the war, the lack of food and other deprivations were wearing people down. Hatred and fear filled the streets of Haifa.

Now heavily pregnant with our second child, I found the temperatures and humidity that July far too oppressive. Suddenly, Khalil came up with the suggestion that we would all go to Nazareth and spend the rest of July and August in the family home. It seemed like an answer from heaven: Nazareth was higher, cooler and not a target for the German air raids. How I thanked God for giving us all a much needed break in the relative safety and fresh air of the countryside: Khalil from the danger zone of the refinery, Siham from the sounds of bombs and sirens, and me from the heat.

That summer the rambling Musallam residence was full of other members of Khalil's family. There were his two unmarried sisters, Radia and Naeema and Kawkab, his half sister and her family from Egypt. In addition to them, there was the Nazareth branch of the family: his stepmother, two half brothers and another half sister, who had their own home but who used to visit us. Rather to my surprise we all got on and, in fact, those summer days of 1941 turned out to be the happiest that I ever spent with my husband and his family.

Another pleasant surprise was that when I contacted the Nazareth hospital about the impending birth, they were willing to accept the transfer of my delivery booking from the hospital in Haifa. When I went for a check up at the hospital, I was told that the doctor who would attend the delivery was none other than a Dr. Hamzeh who had been my midwifery course supervisor during my training. Later, he refused to charge us any fees for the delivery and I was given a private room free of charge, paying only for my food.

On August 18th, 1941 our second daughter was born. I had plenty of visitors while I was in hospital and our new baby girl found no shortage of admirers among them for her beauty and serenity. We gave her the name *Ibtisam* (or 'smiling') and found it most suitable, not just because she smiled, but because every one who looked at her found themselves smiling back.

I can see and feel it all now. I was lying in the stillness of the maternity room, looking out onto a sun-bathed balcony surrounded by pine and cypress trees that barely moved in the afternoon breeze. Aware of almost tangible peacefulness that seemed to envelop the room and stretch out intro the surrounding hills of Galilee beyond, I turned round to look at our wide-awake baby lying in her cot next to my bed and gazed at her large dark and thoughtful eyes in her open face. It was a moment of peace and contentment that, many times in the years ahead, I was to look back on with longing.

Yet the tranquillity was momentary. For one thing, Ibtisam raised issues. My experience with Siham had effectively been of managing her on my own. Now though there was a husband involved and, to cap it all, I was a Christian.

Something of the stress that I felt emerged in a dream where I saw our baby daughter slipping into a muddy hole. I saw my little girl slipping further and further away beyond my reach and I cried desperately for help. Standing by me was my doctor but, as I called out to him to save my daughter, he just laughed and turned away. I woke up from this nightmare in floods of terrified agitation. Urgently I turned to God in prayer and asked him to look after our children: I committed both our daughters to him. Peace returned.

Not every question was so easily submitted to God and resolved. My conversion had not destroyed the old Wadeah, only suppressed her and ever so often, my old stubbornness and selfishness surfaced again. Once more, I found myself saying, 'please no more children'. I had, I confess, little consideration for my husband's wishes and I had not learned to leave this matter in God's hands. Sadly, this particular lesson in obedience was one I never learnt. I bore our children not because I wanted to, but because I had to.

At the end of summer, we left the quiet of Nazareth and returned to our home in Haifa. The air raids seemed more frequent and more intense than they had been and were causing greater damage. Not long after we had returned home, the refinery suffered a direct hit in an air raid. Flames shot up hundreds of feet high into the sky and the resulting pall of smoke and black cloud hung over the city for many weeks before it finally dispersed. With these very literal clouds of war hanging over us, we picked up our life as a small family from where we had left it. Soon even the war became a matter of course and, like everybody else, we carried on with our normal activities as best we could.

The effects of the invaluable and refreshing summer's interlude in Nazareth were gradually worn away by the stresses and hardships of everyday life. Khalil resumed his work at the oil refinery but as his earnings were not sufficient to support our growing family, my midwifery career came into its own again. My old clients and acquaintances were soon aware that I was taking bookings again for home deliveries. Siham started her second year at kindergarten and most days I managed to walk with her to school. On those days when I was out attending to a case, one of my nieces who attended the same school would take Siham with her. Baby Ibtisam found herself looked after either by my mother or sister: they would feed and change her, make sure she was comfortable and put her back in her cot. They spent very little time talking to her or playing with her; she was a very contented baby and made no fuss. On most occasions when I returned home and opened the door, she would be wide-awake and as soon as she heard my voice, she would raise her head supporting herself on her hands and arms and turn towards me with that never-failing bright smile.

One particularly difficult decision I had to make at this time concerned adult baptism. I had begun to attend a Brethren Church which based its teaching and its practices on the New Testament. They held to the principle that baptism was a step which followed conversion, and which was a public witness of an individual's commitment to Christ: it was a symbol of being buried with Christ and rising again to a new life with him. Was I going to be baptised? At first, I was very opposed to the idea. When my brother Nakhleh and his wife who attended the same church let it be known that they were going to be baptised, I opposed their decision with every argument I knew. 'You have already been christened as infants,' I said, 'surely it must be foolishness to do it again.' Of course, I was not really defending any Biblical principle here: I was, instead, trying to avoid and escape a very embarrassing situation. After all, if my brother and his wife were going to be baptised; I might have to follow them. In the end, they were baptised, but I did not attend the service.

Not long after, though, I was persuaded to take this step. After searching in the New Testament and reading all references to baptism, as well as talking to other Christian believers, I became finally convinced that it was one of the basic teachings of God's word and I asked to be baptised. A number of other people in our church also decided to be baptised, so a day was appointed for the service. Not having a baptismal pool in the hall, we all went to a secluded spot along the beach at Haifa, where we were baptised in the sea.

So with God's help I managed to organise our family life and still fit in my outside work too. Yet physically, I was getting overtired and undernourished due to the many shortages. In Spring 1942 I found myself pregnant again.

CHAPTER 9

Births and a Death

Our third child, a daughter, was born on 2nd November 1942. Given the great value that Arab society places on sons, there was great disappointment among both family and friends that we had a third girl. But that tiny baby, born prematurely at the end of the eighth month of pregnancy, was perfect and healthy and she stole our hearts with her doll-like face.

Sadly, Khalil and I had started having rows all over again and the new baby gave us an excuse for another disagreement. Khalil wanted to use his mother's name Afifa, which I objected to, thinking it terribly old fashioned. Khalil though, was adamant and refused to choose another. Time was running out for submitting the birth certificate for our baby daughter and we still had not agreed on a name. Finally, one morning when Khalil was not around, I chose the name 'Ghada' quickly and had the registrar record it on the certificate. My action did not help matters and later, for the sake of peace in our home, a compromise was reached between us, and we agreed to use a particular form of his mother's name, Afaf, which I found more acceptable. Despite the fact that she was born during a war into a quarrelling family, Afaf was always peaceful and contented, a happy baby who grew into a gentle and loving little girl.

Even as Afaf was being born, the fortunes of war were changing. Barely three hundred miles away from the Haifa hospital, the British 8th Army, under General Montgomery, inflicted the first major defeat on the Germans in the war at

El Alamein. Yet while that victory was to ease the German threat to Palestine, it did nothing about the pressing issue of rationing. I was by now constantly tired and placed much of the blame on the lack of nourishing food. I was also under a lot of stress as I had to work outside the home and within it. I found feeding a growing family at a time of such shortages a major worry. Khalil's sisters tried to help but, as before, it merely turned out to be another source of irritation that aggravated our relationship. They would send small gifts of money or food along with such messages as: 'Please use this for our brother, he needs nourishment.' I found these efforts maddening and they eroded every effort to keep peace in our home. Of course, I was hardly blameless: even in later life, I never found accepting charity or handouts easy. But the combination of hard work, poor diet, stress and worry took its toll and my health began steadily deteriorating.

Our growing family had forced us to move to a slightly larger apartment. My eldest brother owned a building next to his house and we rented a vacant first floor flat from him. My parents lived on the ground floor and two families, one Lebanese and the other Jewish, occupied the second floor flats. In spite of the growing tension between Arabs and Jews, there was still a feeling of neighbourliness and security and all our children played together after school.

Khalil now had two jobs. During the weekdays, he worked at the oil refinery but in the evenings and at the weekends he made hand-made shoes in a well-equipped workshop conveniently situated just outside the flat. The demand for his shoes seemed to pick up at this time and the English High School for girls in Haifa placed a large order with him. Khalil was a home loving person; he adored the children and would often come home bearing small gifts and sweets for our girls. They would jump on him before he had a chance to change out of his greasy oil-smelling clothes and, as he sat down to relax after the day's hard work, would scramble up on his knees and shoulders. It was always Ibtisam who got his attention first with her dimpled smile and twinkling eyes while Afaf would snuggle up quietly against him and wait for her turn.

The arrival of Afaf raised the matter of baptism again; in the Anglican church, young children were baptised or 'christened' as infants. By now, I had become fully convinced about the place and meaning of baptism in the Christian life and I felt that baptising infants was futile. Khalil and others in our family still attended the Anglican church in Haifa and neither Ibtisam nor Afaf had yet been christened. Rather than make a fuss about it with Khalil, I simply avoided mentioning the subject in the hope that it would be forgotten. One day, Khalil's sisters came to visit and asked us what arrangements we had made for the girls' christening. I explained my position and belief on the matter, but Khalil insisted he did not agree with me. I had to give in but made it clear that I would not attend the service. I didn't either but I was told the service was a happy one and the girls were as good as gold. I was neither needed nor missed.

The war progressed. The air raids ended and the menace of invasion or attack faded. I became pregnant again and in 1943 had another baby. This time, to universal delight, it was a boy and we called him David. We were almost overwhelmed by the congratulations and the celebrations that we had a boy. Old Aunt Hilaneh, who prayed for many years for this day, came over to Haifa immediately from her home in Shafa 'Amr on hearing the news and walked into the room with tears running down her face. Brother Adib and his wife were up before dawn making the *asideh* and *maghli* – those special sweets that were offered to all who visit the family on such an occasion. There was great excitement and jubilation and I was sure that I had never seen my husband look so happy and proud before. His sisters too were overjoyed at the news. I too was elated and proud. Deep in my heart, I recognised that this boy was a special child for his father and that I would probably have no say in his upbringing.

I was still in the maternity hospital when, dozing off one afternoon, I saw, in a dream, a hand over the baby's cot and a finger pointing directly at him. I woke up extremely disturbed and worried by this experience and could only relate it to my earlier fears and thoughts that I would have no say in his upbringing. So I prayed earnestly, committing our new baby to the Lord yet still no real peace came to me. Instead, a different and worrying thought began to haunt me: that David would grow up to be far away from God. I felt I had no assurance of his future salvation and my spirit fought and contended with God for this child. 'Jesus', I argued with myself, 'is one with God and I am in Christ and so would my son, in me be saved through Christ.' Yet I had no relief from the troubling thought, 'David will follow evil ways and he could go to hell.' In desperation, I cried to God, 'Please take him now, don't allow him to grow up only to suffer and die away from you, without knowing you.'

I was perplexed and alarmed. Why was I saying these things? Did I honestly mean what I said? Did I really expect God to take away his precious gift from us? Was that what I was asking for? My thoughts seemed close to utter madness.

As the months sped by, my unease faded. David grew fast, much faster than the girls had, and had a bigger appetite. By eighteen months, he was well ahead of his age in both size and development. Soon our second daughter, Ibtisam, started school, joining Siham at the English High School. At home, my hands were full with the other two children, as well as the occasional call to do a home delivery. Khalil persevered with his job at the oil refinery, working both day and night shifts.

One afternoon, I went to visit my brother Nakhleh and his wife who were both now committed Christians. It was very enjoyable and refreshing to chat together and 'exchange notes' on our Christian experiences, and to talk about Christian issues and life in general. I had with me Afaf and David: the other two children were at school. As I picked David up out of his pushchair, it struck me that he was not quite himself. He was rather quiet and looked, and felt, feverish. As my face came close to his, I caught the whiff of an ugly smell from his nose that I assumed was a sign of oncoming catarrh. Then he turned to me with a sudden brightening of his eyes and a smile that lit up his whole face and said, 'Bye bye, Mama' before repeating himself, 'Bye bye, Mama'. I reassured myself that children both get ill and recover quickly. Nevertheless, I cut short my visit and we returned home.

But David's condition did not improve: the following day he developed an alarmingly high temperature which brought on severe convulsions. My brother called for the doctor, Sami Musallam, a friend of the family, while Mrs. Zeidan, a neighbour and friend came in to help. Together, we gave David a cold bath, the method then practised to bring down high temperature. My brother returned soon after but without the doctor; Dr. Musallam was unable to attend but, knowing I was a nurse, he had sent a dose of Prontosil, an early antibacterial drug, and I administered the medication. Tragically, it was the wrong decision; David was dehydrated and shouldn't have been given that drug. Had the doctor been there and seen him he would have never treated him with it. David's convulsions increased until his body was wracked with pain and exhaustion. My tears were silently streaming down my face as I held our baby on my lap, feeling that I could not stand his agony any longer. I prayed 'Lord, heal him, make him better or take him to you. But please, oh please, don't let him suffer any longer.' Mrs Zeidan next to me prayed too. Soon David was lying very still and quiet in my arms with a only little sigh and a shudder every now and then to keep alive the hope I had that he might somehow still pull through.

Yet as the night wore on there were no further signs of improvement. My eyes were burning with crying and sleeplessness. I turned my face away from my son and tried to close my aching eyes and as I did I seemed to meet God's comforting gaze and see his arms surrounding me and my son. His look seemed to say 'Can you now begin to understand what I felt when I saw my Son hanging on the Cross for you and the whole world? I love my Son, I love you, and I love your son. Trust me always.'

When the doctor finally arrived, it was all over.

The following day, after an autopsy, the funeral was arranged and David our treasured son was buried in the local Protestant cemetery in Haifa. We believe he is still our treasure in heaven waiting for the great reunion through our Lord Jesus Christ.

Slowly, our mourning hearts for David were comforted and life continued its relentless onward journey. We had plenty to occupy ourselves: our three young daughters were growing fast and were healthy, strong and active. These final war years were tough years economically. The fighting might have been a long way away by now but there were still shortages. The government imposed strict price controls on most foodstuffs but the result was that, rather than sell goods at the cheaper government prices, retailers, simply chose to sell them on the black market. Many Christians were faced with a dilemma: did they follow government rules and find no food to eat, or break the law and have plenty? I chose the first alternative and on more than one occasion, incurred my husband's wrath because we had no meat for a few days.

There were other problems. As the end of the war came in sight, the issue of the future of Palestine was emerging again. Thousands more Jews were entering into the country, both legally and illegally and the Palestinian Arabs felt helpless to do anything about it. With the impending end of Second World War, all the old issues to do with Palestine that had been partially buried since 1939 now boiled up again. The Zionist organisations, which had supported Britain against fascism during the war, now felt free to attack their old ally; from 1944 Jewish terror attacks against the British began with the clear intent of driving them out.

Jobs were becoming scarcer and there was growing unrest: rumours and counter-rumours were rife. A major employer of technical, mechanical and other workforce was the Iraqi Petroleum Company whose oil pipeline reached an oil line terminal at Haifa. Just before the end of the war, the site sustained a direct hit from a German bomber that turned the whole place into an inferno, with flames reaching high into the sky and smoke covering the city for weeks. Hundreds of their employees were laid off. At that time, three members of our family worked there: my husband and my two brothers. Gradually the refinery recovered and workers slowly returned but many Arabs found that Jews had taken their jobs.

Late in 1944, I found I was pregnant again and on the 17th May 1945, I gave birth to another daughter. I was not disappointed. We named our new daughter Huda and, like her sisters and her brother, she was committed to the Lord for his care and love. Khalil too, found comfort with the new baby. Yet there was a brief moment of tears for both of us as we returned home from the maternity hospital and placed Huda in the cot that had last been used by our dear son David.

Huda's birth came just ten days after the end of the Second World War in Europe. With peace at last and a new baby, the future might have appeared rosy. But, once more, trouble was on its way.

Early picture of the family. Wadeah back row, second from right.

Wadeah with her first daughter in Haifa.

Wadeah with her first grandchild in Beirut.

Wadeah with three older daughters.

The author, Siham Brown.

CHAPTER 10

Struggles at Home

Sadly, our marriage had by now become increasingly unhappy. The pain of David's death and the joy of Huda's birth had brought only brief spells of unity in what was now a dangerously fragmented relationship. Soon our home life started to disintegrate in a rapid and most alarming fashion and there were often almost complete breakdowns in communication between my husband and me. Khalil had no interest in my life, either inside, or outside the home, and I was cut off from his life at work. Days and even weeks, would pass without us exchanging a single word. As ever, I found the input of Khalil's family unhelpful. His sisters would often send gifts and messages for the children, give invitations for us to visit them, or make enquiries about the health of one of the children – but as far as they were concerned, I did not exist.

My response to these situations was often to adopt an attitude of complete detachment. If Khalil decided to take the children out without consulting me, then I let him see to all the details of getting them ready, washed and dressed. I refused to get involved; if I did, it was inevitable that my feelings smouldered and then flared up. The result then would be a full-blown row with recrimination, ugly words and even blows. Later, when I was alone and in the quietness of the house, I would moan through my tears and prayers at the burden I was carrying and the hardships I was putting up with. I felt quite unable to take my husband as he was, including his weaknesses and shortcomings. I wanted him to change and become my idea of a man and husband. As ever, I was blind to the fact that these principles of being changed also applied to me too. The idea that *I* could change and adapt was not a thought that naturally occurred to me.

By now, our relationship had deteriorated so much that we were not in control of our married life any more; we seemed to be carried along on a current of self-destruction. Incidents flared up, erupted and then cooled down, but each time the solid impenetrable barrier between us was that bit harder, thicker and higher than it had been before. And this growing wall blocked out hearing, seeing and feeling what the other felt. I turned to God in my prayers as the only and last resort, telling him that I couldn't stand it any longer, that I couldn't take any more. How I expected God to intervene in our life, I had no idea.

Apart from God, and the fellowship I had with other Christians, the one thing that kept me going was my work as a midwife. Yet it was physically exhausting and mentally demanding. It also required that I be ready to leave my home and children whenever the call came to attend to one of my cases. And with the deteriorating security situation, being out, especially at night, became ever riskier.

With the ending of the Second World War on the ground, what had been sporadic clashes between Arabs and Jews became almost permanent battles. When the confrontations worsened, the British imposed frequent curfews although as a midwife I was given a special permit to allow me to travel at night. Night calls were often very scaring and I would feel my heart pounding with fear as I walked along dark and deserted streets hearing gunfire. Other times, I would find myself walking along with my hand over my head, as if that would protect me from bullets and shells. When I neared home, I would begin to run and dash into our apartment, exhausted and terrified but thanking God for my safe return home. Fortunately, with my parents living on the ground floor of the same building, there was no problem finding a baby sitter if I had to go out unexpectedly when Khalil wasn't in. Once, when I was out, the guns sounded too close for comfort and my mother panicked. She grabbed hold of the two older girls, Siham and Ibtisam, dashed out of our apartment and ran downstairs with them, thinking they would all be safer there. She forgot the baby, Afaf, asleep in her cot!

God did not desert us during those trying times. Although I was largely unaware of his presence, I know he was there at every stage, supporting, teaching, and moulding me into the person that he wanted me to be. Faced with so many problems, I found Christian fellowship particularly valuable. On Sundays, I would attend the morning service at our meeting place, the local Brethren Assembly, accompanied by the girls who would go to Sunday School. Khalil never joined us, preferring to go with his sisters to the Anglican Church. There were also weekday evening meetings that I seldom missed. My attendance here brought down harsh criticism on me from Khalil, his sisters and my own family; they called me 'mad' and accused me of neglecting my children and husband. Nevertheless, I managed to fulfil all my duties at home towards our children and my husband. Somehow, I would prepare a cooked dinner, feed the children, bathe them, get them ready for bed, and still manage to get to the meetings.

I believe that one of the hardest lessons God was trying to teach me in those days was to accept his will in my life. As we studied the Lord's Prayer at a series of meetings, I was struck by the phrase 'thy will be done on earth as it is in heaven'. I felt I could not honestly say this particular verse because, all too often, it was my own will that I wanted to be done. Frankly, I wonder whether even now, in my 80s, I have learned to do his will completely. Even now, when people tell me that I'm wrong and they're right or that my memory has failed me on some fact, my old stubborn will rises up and wants to argue!

By the middle of 1946, the Zionist attacks on the British

reached a new level of ferocity. In July of that year, the King David Hotel in Jerusalem, which had become the headquarters of the British military command in Palestine, was bombed by a Jewish terrorist group organisation with the loss of nearly a hundred lives. There were almost daily attacks against the British forces, and it soon became plain that far from wishing to sort out the Palestinian problem, the British – exhausted by the World War and disillusioned about the possibility of making any sort of lasting settlement in Palestine – were looking for a way out. Knowing the British were no longer committed to staying simply encouraged the Zionists to more acts of terror against them. The crisis deepened.

Everywhere, families prayed for the safety of their men folk at work and their safe return home evening by evening. Khalil's job at the refinery was however still secure and he appreciated having a regular job and income when many had lost both. It was at this time, Khalil's health began to give rise for concern. He developed a slight but constant cough that caused him a lot of discomfort and made him very irritable. He consulted a chest specialist who, after taking some x-rays, diagnosed a non-malignant cyst between the lungs and the diaphragm. The consultant was not unduly worried and reassured us that the cyst could be removed as soon as it adhered to the wall of the chest but that, as it was still floating, he couldn't advise surgery. The consultant did mention the possibility of an internal rupture and bleeding as a result of pressure from the cyst on the lungs, but said that if that happened the matter could be dealt with in hospital. There was, he reassured us, no undue cause for worry or alarm: all Khalil needed to do was to keep in good general health.

There were now new tensions in our marriage. For some weeks, the only topic Khalil and I seemed to talk about was his planned visit to his sister Kawkab in Egypt. I had no objections until he mentioned taking all the girls with him.

This was something that, under the British rules, required my consent because they were on my passport. I tried to reason with Khalil explaining that, because of their young age (Huda wasn't yet a year old) I wouldn't dream of letting them go without me. Khalil's stubborn answer was that *he* was their father and that he would be with them all the time. Besides, he added, his sister would look after them too. Alarm bells rang very loudly. I knew for certain that if the girls left with their father for Egypt, I would never see them again. I refused to give my passport to my husband, assuming that this would be the end of the matter. It wasn't: Khalil's next plan was to go to Cairo alone.

I then heard a slightly different story from my brother Halim; Khalil had informed him that he was leaving us for good. Halim was concerned about Khalil's responsibility towards my children and was anxious that I should come to some agreement with my husband over financial support for the family. I understood his concern but, perhaps strangely, I had no desire to take the matter any further or do any more. All I wanted was to have this chapter of my life closed.

It was obvious that my husband and I had reached the end of the road together. I found myself getting worried about the future and wondering uneasily as to what might happen to us. As I was resting on my bed, one evening, not quite asleep and feeling exhausted and sad, I suddenly seemed to be in a vast hospital building. I was aware that my husband was there and very ill. I discovered which ward he was in and was on the point of going in to see him, when his two sisters appeared at the door. They would not let me in: I was crying and begging them to let me see him, but to no avail. One of them even pushed me away and kicked me with her foot. I woke up from my daydream and wondered at the silliness of imagining all this when my husband was in good health.

A few days later, Khalil got up early in the morning to prepare for going to work. He made his sandwiches, had his cup of tea and left the house. Being awake too, I found myself listening to his footsteps as he went out of the front door, round the side of the house, past the bedroom windows and then down the hilly path before dying away in the distance. Wondering why I did so, I strained my ears to hear the last footstep.

Within the hour, my youngest brother came running up to the house to tell me that Khalil had had an accident and had been taken to hospital. Leaving the children at home, I immediately got into a taxi with my brother and went straight to the hospital. We dashed to the emergency room where I found Khalil still lying on the stretcher. There were no signs of any of the injuries I had imagined from the message I received. I called out to the nurses, 'Please do something! Why isn't anyone attending to Khalil?' A young doctor came up to me, put a kindly hand on my shoulder and told me that he was already dead.

Eventually, I pieced together what had happened. Khalil had been waiting as usual with a small group of workers for the company bus. As the men had boarded the bus, Khalil had slipped, hit the lower part of his chest against the sharp edge of the bus step and passed out. The bus driver had quickly phoned for an ambulance on his emergency telephone and Khalil had been taken to the main hospital in Haifa. Meanwhile a refinery employee on the bus, who had seen what had happened, returned to my parents' house and gave them the news of Khalil's accident. The autopsy explained the medical facts. The non-malignant cyst we had known about had grown so large that it had ruptured the lungs and caused internal bleeding. The autopsy couldn't ascertain whether the rupture of the lung was the cause, or the effect, of Khalil's fall. It didn't really matter: the fact was that he was dead.

The days of mourning and grief for Khalil were painful and devastating. For all my problems with him, he had still been my husband. The fact that my relationship with his family was strained to the utmost didn't help matters either. They had blamed me for his ill health and now I found that I was blamed for his death too.

These early days of widowhood seemed to stretch out for ever. There was little to distract me: the uncertainty of the political situation had resulted in the schools being closed and I had very little work. In those long sad and empty days, I found myself frequently revisiting the past, walking through the alleyways and lanes of my memory, trying to make sense of the events and trying to glean some encouragement for the future. As I pondered past events, I remembered two incidents which had happened only days before Khalil died. At the time, they had been neither strange nor striking, but now they seemed both.

In the evening before the day Khalil died, we had all been in the sitting room when Afaf, then five years old, had said in a loud voice 'Mummy, Daddy's going to heaven, isn't he?' 'Yes, darling" I had replied. 'He will go to heaven.' Then, as though not quite certain yet, she continued talking to herself: 'We'll pray for him.' The next day he was dead.

The other strange incident had happened a few weeks before Khalil died and puzzled me because it seemed not to have come true. As I was going round the house, doing my housework room by room, I found that a persistent thought kept running through my mind. It was that Khalil would be leaving us soon; perhaps going to Cairo to his sister's family for good. As I struggled with the thought, my eyes kept wandering over the various objects and furniture in the house, imagining that Khalil would be taking this or that item. I found myself struggling with parting with so many of those possessions that had become so much part of our life as a family. Soon afterwards, I even started putting away on one side those things that I expected Khalil to want to take with him. Coming to terms with the idea of losing so many items was very hard. Finally, after much prayer and commitment to the Lord, the bitterness and blame that had built up in my heart started gradually melting away. Now, in the days immediately after Khalil's death, these thoughts puzzled me and I found myself wondering at the feelings I experienced. Why, I asked, had God allow me to imagine something that hadn't happened?

Within months, I was to find out the answer.

CHAPTER 11

Leaving my land

By the summer of 1947, bomb explosions and deaths were occurring almost daily in Haifa. In July members of the Jewish Irgun terrorist group kidnapped, and then hung, two British Army sergeants. The resulting outrage greatly weakened the already feeble British resolve and they handed the fate of Palestine over to the infant United Nations.

In November 1947, the UN debated the matter of Palestine and, after intense American pressure, passed Resolution 181, which divided Palestine into two approximately equal portions, a Jewish state of Israel and an Arab state of Palestine. Given that only about 8% of the land was owned by Jews or the Jewish Agency and that Jews represented only one third of the population, the resolution was rejected by Arabs.

On the 30th of December 1947, Jewish terrorists carried out a bomb attack against a crowd of several hundred Arabs at the main gate of the Haifa oil refinery, where they were waiting in the hope of work. Six were killed and many others were injured. The next morning, a group of militant, aggressive Arab workers secretly armed themselves with any metallic object they could lay their hands on, entered one of the large work sheds in the refinery, locked the door behind them, and attacked the unsuspecting Jewish workers. The outcome was a full-scale massacre that resulted in the killing of over forty Jews. Zionist retaliation followed swiftly, with the killing of close to sixty innocent men, women, and children in the village of Balad al-Shaykh just outside Haifa. For the first time – but not the last – civilians were massacred.

In the first few weeks of 1948, what was effectively civil war erupted between Jews and Arabs: two peoples fighting to the death to keep what each considered its rightful ownership of the homeland. Haifa soon split up into a series of Jewish and Arab neighbourhoods separated by dangerous strips of no-man's land. Zionist attacks increased with the clear goal of forcing the Arab population to leave. Under the impact of these attacks, by the end of January 1948, around 20,000 Arabs fled Haifa. The British were unable to control the situation and seemed to be packing their trunks ready to leave. Many Palestinians were openly encouraged to leave the country, 'Take a holiday, just for a short time,' they were told by the British, 'for a few weeks, just until things quieten down and some form of government emerges.' With no street in Haifa now safe from stray bullets, families didn't need much encouragement to leave.

On the 29th of February 1948, the Zionists rolled down large oil drums filled with explosives from a Jewish neighbourhood of Haifa into an Arab neighbourhood, which resulted in massive devastation of that residential area. More Arabs fled soon after this incident.

The Habiby family began to leave. Wadii and his family went to Cairo; Adib, Karim and Halim and their families went to Damascus and Naim took our elderly parents back to their village of Shafa 'Amr before continuing himself on to Egypt. Emile, his wife and baby daughter went to Ramallah about ten miles north of Jerusalem while and my sister Nada, her husband and twin daughters, found refuge in Nazareth. Of the Hababys, only Nakhleh, our families, and I stayed in Haifa. Nakhleh and his family left their apartment in the centre of town and, bringing just a few essentials, came to live next to me, renting one of the vacant flats in brother Wadii's house. His wife Afaf, was pregnant and the baby due any day: when the time came, I delivered a beautiful baby daughter; Rhoda.

Soon our neighbours had left as well and the street outside our house had become deserted; at night we could hear the jackals howling just outside our houses. The paths were overgrown with weeds and tall grass: no one walked them any more.

Meanwhile the fighting was escalating and the sound of firearms was increasingly that of a full-scale battle: large calibre guns, machine guns, cannons and bombs. The incessant noise pounded our ears, pummelled our brains and tortured our nerves. The death toll mounted but it was impossible to know the figures: many of those who were killed lay where they fell in dark alleys, unidentified and soon forgotten except by their families and loved ones.

A few minutes walk from our house, just down Abbas Street, past the Carmelite school for girls with its high walls, was the corner shop from which we bought most of our provisions of basic foodstuffs and household needs. One day, its kindly middle-aged Italian owner, Manuel, was blown up, his body smashed beyond recognition in the town centre, as he tried to buy goods to restock his shop. His shop closed and we had very little left to live on.

At that time, a cousin of mine, Violet Habiby was staying in the home of Dr. and Mrs. Churchur. It turned out that Dr Churchur needed a nurse to help him in his clinic; Violet mentioned this to me and I was taken on. I was glad of the much-needed money but the fresh vegetables from Mrs. Churchur's kitchen garden were an extra heaven-sent bonus. One day we had some marrows, another some corn, still another, a few tomatoes or a cucumber.

Nakhleh, Afaf and I missed the Christian fellowship at the Assembly Hall. It was now simply too dangerous to travel from one district to another: local buses had almost come to a standstill. Anyway, most of the original founding members of our church had also already left Haifa by now, most going to Lebanon. Increasingly, the three of us came to realise that, short of a miraculous change in the political situation, we were not going to be able to stay in Haifa much longer. And no such miracle seemed likely. Where would we go? And how could we travel? We had six children and a baby who was barely one month old. The simple answer was, we felt, that we couldn't go anywhere. We were trapped in a nightmare.

One evening in early April, I was called out to a delivery case. It was too early for curfew so I did not take my pass with me and the husband of the expectant mother drove me to the house. On examining the mother, I realized that she wouldn't deliver for a few hours. The husband begged me to stay but I insisted on returning home to my children. By then the curfew had started and the husband couldn't drive me home, so I walked. I hadn't gone far before I was stopped by a policeman who was going to arrest me because I had no pass. When I explained my predicament to him and told him about my children, the policeman was sympathetic and gave me a lift home in his car instead! When, the following day, the baby did arrive, I was in attendance.

On April 9, 1948, two Jewish terror groups attacked the village of Deir Yassin near Jerusalem, which had a peace pact with its Jewish neighbours, and massacred over a hundred Arab civilians. Word of the massacre spread among the Arabs and many who had intended staying, now had second thoughts. By mid April, the battle for Haifa had begun in earnest. It was now obvious that we too needed to leave: but how?

The answer to our prayers and a solution to our problem came from an unexpected quarter. A cousin, the Reverend Rafik Farah, a minister in the Anglican Church in Haifa, came to see us one day with an urgent message. There was a convoy of British Army trucks leaving Haifa the following morning for Jordan and going at least as far as the border. As well as taking the women and children who had been driven from their homes by the Jews, the British were offering to take a few families with them. There was no time for discussing the matter: our desperate circumstances made up our minds for us. We accepted the offer. Nakhleh and my daughter Siham took down a few belongings, including two mattresses to the pick up point outside St. Luke's School.

Early the following morning, we all walked down to join the rest of the group. Nakhleh and his family had one large suitcase and I had one medium sized case; I had packed enough clothing in it for my children and myself to last a fortnight! I remember how Afaf and I had a wordless struggle over a beautiful antique Red Riding Hood doll. Without a word, Afaf, who was just six, took the doll out of its drawer and placed it on the suitcase. Equally silently, I placed it back in its drawer. In no time, Afaf brought it out again and this time placed it inside the suitcase. Sadly, but firmly, I returned the doll once more to its bed in the drawer. I explained to Afaf that we would find her safe and happy when we returned. I was not to know that we were to lose everything; including the doll. It was to be forty years before I saw that house again: and that was only to be a fleeting visit.

The army trucks were already loaded with the women, children and a few old men from the surrounding villages. There was an eerie atmosphere of dazed numbness and uneasy quietness and if anyone spoke, it was in hushed tones. Our few belongings were stacked on one of the trucks with us; the two mattresses, rolled up in one corner formed a fairly comfortable seating area for us. And so we set off into the unknown.

The first stop was made in Rafidiyeh, a small village just outside Nablus, where some passengers got off. Next we were taken to Nablus where the convoy stopped. Suddenly, we were told to get down from the trucks. There were new orders; we had to make our own way to Jordan.

As if in a trance, we disembarked and stood by the side of the road next to our belongings. The late afternoon sun cast long weary shadows, a reflection of what we felt in our hearts. In desperation, it occurred to me that I had done part of my nursing training in Nablus Government Hospital. But that had been some years ago and getting to the hospital was not going to be easy. Armed Palestinians were everywhere, patrolling the streets and everyone knew that it was only a matter of time before the Jews attacked and drove the residents out of their homes here as they had done elsewhere. Our only hope was to get to Jordan as soon as possible. But how?

Suddenly a man appeared from nowhere. He was a truck owner and asked if we wanted to go to Amman. He was taking as many as his vehicle would hold and was charging three Palestinian pounds per family. We thanked God and accepted. Later we were to discover that it was the mayor of Nablus who had organized the transport.

Packed with its human cargo the open truck rattled and swayed, in the growing evening gloom as it hurtled through the wild hills and mountains down into the Jordan valley and up the other side. I knew the route and thanked God that, in the darkness of the night, we couldn't see either the narrow winding road with its hairpin bends or the sheer drops of hundreds of feet down the side. Soon utter exhaustion and sleepiness overtook everyone; heads lolled from side to side until eventually bodies just slumped against each other. In the gloom, I could glimpse my poor sister-in-law with her month-old baby in her arms looking more dead than alive. Yet somehow I stayed awake, my hands tightly clasped with fear and anxiety. I prayed incessantly to God to see us through safely to Amman.

God answered that prayer. The truck didn't break down and we were received by some policemen in Amman city centre. Their orders were to take all refugees to a camp just outside the city. My brother explained that we were meeting some friends the following day and needed to stay in town. It was now past midnight and neither Nakhleh nor I knew Amman. One of the policemen assured us that it was impossible to find anywhere to stay that night and not just because of the lateness of the hour: the city had been overwhelmed by thousands of Palestinian refugees. No relative, friend, or acquaintance had any rooms left unoccupied. Then, his heart evidently softened at the sight of six exhausted children and a tiny baby, the policeman said 'Come with me.' We followed him with our bits and pieces of luggage, walking as if we were in a dream, and stopped outside a tall building. The building was in darkness; something which was explained when we saw that it was no more than a part-built concrete shell. We climbed the stairs and found an empty room. Siham and Ibtisam wandered off, going from one room to another, investigating what was 'round the corner'. I went after them; following them from the sound of their voices and found them peering into the darkness of what seemed to be another room. Taking them each by the hand, I returned to our 'room' where the others were. As I tried to get the children to sleep, Nakhleh mentioned that he had filled in the entry forms for all of us and had registered us with the police as 'Palestinian refugees'. For the first time the fact that my family and I were now refugees sank into my tired mind. Then, in what was left of the night, we slept and God gave us a most peaceful and complete rest.

The first task to face with the following morning was getting in touch with some of the friends in the Brethren Churches living in Amman in the hope of finding a place to live. Nakhleh went off to deal with that, while the rest of us got packed and awaited his return. For breakfast, I was able to buy a round of *kaak b'simsum* each – a delicious freshly baked sesame bread cake off the stall of a street vendor. Another small mercy was discovering a toilet on our floor that had been installed for the workmen.

Surveying the uncompleted flat that we were in, I came to the place where I had found my two daughters peering into the dark space the night before. I suddenly stopped dead, frozen with terror. Just in front of where they had stood was an open gap with a drop of some fifty feet to the street below. One more step and my two daughters would have fallen to their certain death. From that moment, I felt assured that God had joined us in our stay in Jordan and beyond and would keep a watchful eye on each of us. It was no more 'me and my children', rather, it was 'Jesus, me and my children'.

Somehow, things seemed a lot brighter.

CHAPTER 12

Jordan

We stayed in the unfinished building for three days. Finally, thanks to a Christian friend, Saleem Kewar, we found somewhere. Saleem was a major in the Jordanian army and sent one of his assistants with my brother to help him search the city for somewhere for us to stay. The Amman of 1948 bore no resemblance to the present day Amman with its modern buildings and affluent suburbs surrounded with beautiful gardens and tree lined streets. The centre of the city lay at the bottom of a steep-sided valley. The residential areas clustered on the valley slopes so that to get to a house from the city centre almost always involved a climb of hundreds of steps. To those of us who had lived in the sophistication of Haifa, Amman seemed a poor and backward place on the edge of the desert.

On the third day, Nakhleh and his friend found us a single room. It was big enough to sleep ten people but that was all: there was no bath, no kitchen and no toilet. In the courtyard, a short distance from our room was a toilet that was shared by the other families and a tap that we could use to get water. The walls and ceiling of the room were whitewashed and smelt of clean, fresh straw and the floor was pressed earth.

I comforted myself with the thought that we would only stay there until something better turned up. It took only one night to realize how urgent that need for 'something better' was. In the morning, the children – indeed all of us – were covered from head to toe with red spots. Behind the whitewash, the walls were infested with bugs, which had feasted on us during the night.

Getting a bath was not as hard as it might have seemed as Amman had no shortage of public Turkish baths, which were both plentiful and cheap. They were beautifully constructed and lined with ornate marble inside and out and there we enjoyed the hot water to our heart's content and all of us came out sparkling clean.

Our landlady was a middle-aged woman from Salt, a small town northwest of Amman. Every morning, we would find her in the courtyard seated in the same spot, dressed in black from her head to her feet, smoking a pipe that reached down to her toes. She was rather aloof but when she did speak, her voice echoed as if from the depth of a cave. When, driven by the bugs, we finally found somewhere else to stay and told her we were moving, she must have been disappointed but she said nothing, acknowledging our words with only a nod of her head.

Our new home was one of three newly built concrete houses in a row and it had a proper floor and the luxury of an additional small room. A long open space stretched in front of all three houses. Our tiny apartment had an outside toilet and we obtained water by filling water in buckets and jugs from an outside standpipe. Our small extra room doubled up as a cooking space and somewhere for us to wash.

One redeeming feature of our new accommodation was that we only had to walk down the hill, cross the small stream at the bottom of the valley on stepping-stones, walk a few yards further on and we were at the Brethren assembly hall. There we met together on Sundays with other church members for prayer and worship. Many families in the church helped us as best they could; inviting us in for meals and making us feel welcome among them.

We had expected to be in Jordan for just two weeks and considered our refugee status to be a temporary matter. However, back in Palestine, nothing was being resolved; or at least nothing that would allow us to return. On May 14, 1948, the Jews proclaimed the independent State of Israel, and the British immediately withdrew from Palestine. The next day, neighbouring Arab nations attacked Israel but, through a failure to organize and unite, they lost the advantage that they had of superior numbers. Israel lost control of east Jerusalem to Jordan but survived. In fact, the results of the 1948 war were catastrophic for Palestinians. When the fighting ended, Israel held even more land than the UN had granted it (around 78% of the area west of the Jordan river) and about 780,000 Arabs had fled or been driven out of Israel and became refugees in neighbouring Arab countries. The refusal of the Arab countries to sign a permanent peace treaty with Israel meant that the Palestinian refugees stayed in a legal limbo. Fifty years later, many were still in refugee camps.

Slowly our fortnight 'holiday' stretched on and soon the summer season was upon us with its oppressive heat. Baby Rhoda was often placed in her wicker cot in a shady corner just outside the front door for some fresh air. One afternoon, as she lay there peacefully asleep, Ibtisam came running inside to tell me and her aunt that there was a 'worm' in the baby's cot next to her face. We ran out and as we looked into the cot, we almost stopped breathing: there, with its tail curved up ready to strike at the slightest disturbance or sound, was an adult scorpion, yellow with poison, In one swift movement, Afaf shook the scorpion off the cot sheet and, as it scuttled away, I managed to kill it.

That summer news came that my father had died but there was nothing that I could do other than weep and, by roundabout means of communication, send condolences to my mother. In those increasingly desperate days, we gave God no rest as we constantly cried out to him with our needs. With our stay away from home stretching out into the future, I tried to find employment. I tried every avenue, followed every suggestion and listened to every bit of advice yet all without any success. The only one hospital job I was offered was a night shift one but with four young daughters and a one-room home, I found myself having to refuse it.

Once, my second daughter, Ibtisam, developed a debilitating strain of dysentery and started losing blood. I was certain she would die without the right medicine and treatment. At the same time Huda, our youngest, developed a skin disease so that her whole body was covered with infected sores. Both children needed medicine but that cost money that I did not have. I had already sold my wedding ring a few days earlier in order to buy a hypodermic syringe and needles so that I could work as a private nurse and give injections but I had nothing to help my sick children. On hearing of our problems, Roy Whitman, the leader of our church, came over immediately and prayed for our two girls. Through his encouragement and faith, I too came to believe that God could still do miracles. Indeed, two miracles were just what he did do. The next morning Ibtisam seemed brighter: she was feeling hungry and her bleeding had stopped while Huda's sores appeared to have dried up during the night. The healing was soon complete and the diseases did not recur.

From time to time, friends and acquaintances called on me to give injections and do small nursing jobs: that was a great help, although the fees involved were small. I was interviewed for a housekeeper's job in the home of a government minister but they wanted someone to live in; so yet again, another door closed. Nakhleh, a mechanical engineer, found a job at the airport but it didn't last long and he was out of work again. Our money was running out fast and very little was coming in to replace it. We seemed to be sinking further into trouble.

One day, we were told that free bread was being given daily to all registered refugees, so Siham went along to get some. By noon, she still hadn't returned home and I couldn't wait any longer. I left the other three girls at home with my sister-in-law and almost ran all the way to the distribution centre. My little daughter was still standing in a queue, with a large tear in one of her sleeves, the result, I presumed, of a struggle to keep her place in the queue. I went no further: I lifted my face and heart to God in heaven, and challenged him: 'You promised to be a father to my children: is this the kind of fatherhood you were offering them?' Then, my eyes blinded with tears, I turned round and returned home without my daughter seeing me.

What I really needed, I reasoned, was to find a boarding school that was willing to take all my daughters, leaving me free to find a good job with a salary adequate to pay for my daughters' schooling. I valued schooling very highly. There were other opinions however: one well-meaning friend implied in a comment that it was more important to feed the children than to worry about their education.

As before, the Whitmans came to my rescue. They knew of a couple of mission schools in Lebanon and suggested I write to my cousin Munir who had moved to Lebanon in order to enquire on my behalf, whether there was any possibility of my daughters attending one of their schools. I did, but no reply came from Munir! He never got the letter. Yet despite this silence, the idea of those Christian schools in Lebanon gripped me like a vice and wouldn't let go. In the darkness that I was in, it seemed like a flame burning inside me, night and day: I was determined to pursue this quest to its fulfilment.

By now though, time was short. September was almost over and the schools were starting to open. My days and nights turned into one long prayer for my children and for us as a family. When I moaned about our living situation, my brother Nakhleh would often remind me to be grateful: 'At least we have a roof over our heads when many others are still living in tents; you should thank God for this house!'

My response, I'm afraid, was not very reverent: full of fury I turned to my brother and said 'I will *not* thank God for this house. It is unworthy of him to give it to any child of His! I shall insist on something better.'

One day, I remembered that Dora Whitman had mentioned to me that a cousin of hers, Pauline Stammers, was a member of the British Syrian Mission, a missionary society working in Lebanon and elsewhere. I begged Dora to write to her cousin about the schools in Lebanon. Dora explained that her cousin was in Damascus in Syria, but that she knew of another lady missionary in Lebanon who was the principal of a recently opened school in Baalbek. She would, she said, write to her.

That evening, my brother and sister-in-law went to a church meeting. Mentally and physically exhausted from the battle going on within me, I decided to stay at home. Our children were already in bed and asleep and I stretched out on the mattress beside them to rest. I dozed off for a short while then woke up and felt an urgent need to pray. Siham was lying asleep next to me: gently, I woke her up and asked her if she would pray with me. We both sat upright on the mattress, and I opened my Bible to read a verse and my eyes fastened on Philippians chapter 3 verse 1, 'Finally, my brothers, rejoice in the Lord.'

I didn't read any further: I couldn't. Something like a strong gust of wind flung my daughter and me sideways, stretching us out full length on the floor. We were both crying and laughing simultaneously and the only meaningful words we could hear each other saying were 'Thank you, Lord Jesus' repeated over and over again. Eventually, our sobs subsided and, still dazed from our experience, we sat up. I turned to my daughter, gave her a big hug and told her that our problems in Amman were over: God had answered our prayers. From tomorrow, I said, we'll start getting ready.

For what? How? When? I realised I had no answer to any of these questions, but I didn't care: I knew that God would take care of the details. All I knew was that our sufferings and hardships in Amman were over.

Later, I found out what had happened a hundred and fifty miles away in Lebanon that same evening. The British Syrian Mission had had a school in Ain Zahlta, a small village in the Chouf mountains region of Lebanon for many years. Then for several reasons, including very low numbers, the mission had decided to move the school with its staff to Baalbek in the northern Bekaa valley of Lebanon and a missionary, Miss Freda Button, had been appointed principal of the new boarding school. Teachers, both old and new, had already arrived for the school, as had the cook from Ain Zahlta. But as the boarders had arrived with their suitcases and trunks, a problem had emerged. There was no matron for the boarding department and no one either free, or able, to look after the girls. There had been a few applicants for the post but all had been found unsuitable. The mission management were desperate to find a matron and the very evening that Siham and I had prayed, the request at the staff prayer meeting was for God to 'please send us the right person; a Christian lady both capable and committed to the work.'

The next morning, Dora Whitman's letter to Freda Button arrived in the post asking if the school could use Wadeah Musallam: a Christian lady and a trained nurse. In Amman, that morning I woke up still full of assurance and confidence that the Lord had answered our prayer and that a way would open up for us. I knew that the previous night's experience had not been a dream: I knew it had been a genuine meeting with God in the person of the Holy Spirit. For the next few days, we were living in a high state of expectancy. There was absolutely nothing to say or talk about: just an inner excitement so deep that it almost turned into an ache!

It was still warm enough to sit outside on the terrace in front of the house where Afaf and I could watch the children play. Suddenly Nakhleh, who had gone to the town, came up the lane, half walking, half running and waving something in his hand that looked like a piece of white paper.

'It's for you, Wadeah,' he called out. 'A telegram!'

The telegram had come to us via the Whitman's address. My brother could hardly contain himself and my hands barely stopped shaking as I read what it said. The only problem was that it didn't make sense: the Arabic said 'Accepting

Wadeah and her father to Baalbek. My journey will follow.' I didn't understand: my father was already dead and whose journey did it refer to? Nakhleh suggested taking the telegram back to the post office where the original message could be checked. There light dawned: the telegram should have read, 'Wadeah and her children accepted in Baalbek. My letter will follow.' In written Arabic, the words for *father* and *children* and *letter* and *journey* are similar enough to be easily confused.

I thanked God from the bottom of my heart, but hard on the heels of my praise, came new worries. There were long lists of items that the children and I needed. As I listed them in my mind, I wondered how I would find the money to buy even the essential items. It was hard to think rationally about anything: what had happened to us was just too overwhelming. In the end, I realised that there were no answers; I could only trust that the God who had open this door would supply our needs.

Within days, Freda Button's letter arrived. It was clear and set out the picture concisely and methodically. There was however, one unmistakeable and painful condition of acceptance. Huda my youngest daughter, who was only three years old, could not be accepted. She was too young for school and would only get in the way of accomplishing my daily tasks and routine. It was a condition that was non-negotiable.

As I realised what my family and I were embarking on, I had a sick feeling in the pit of my stomach. It was an enormous challenge and I felt weak at the thought of it. Yet here again, I felt myself totally dependent on the Lord our God. I knew he wouldn't let us down.

My first plan was to go to Damascus, where three of my brothers and their families were now living. I would stay a few days there to buy clothes and other necessities for the children and, if possible, arrange for Huda to stay with them. I would then travel on to Baalbek; a three hour journey by car. As I prepared to leave, many of our friends from the Amman church helped us with various gifts of money, and other useful items. Baalbek is over 3000 feet above sea level and its reputation for being cold in winter was well known even in Amman so there were also welcome presents of warm clothing.

But how to get to Damascus? The best way would be by hiring a taxi; my daughters and I would fill one. That, though, was out of the question, as we could not afford it. I became reconciled to the idea of the long, tiring, but affordable, bus journey. The following morning we sat outside to make some definite plans for the journey when I was surprised to see someone who looked like my brother Karim, who lived in Damascus with his family, coming up the hill. The man turned off the path and came towards the house: it *was* Karim!

I was overjoyed at seeing my brother. He and his family had left Haifa before us and I hadn't seen him for months. Over coffee and then lunch, he brought us up to date with the news of the family in Damascus. He now ran a successful taxi service business, employing five or six drivers, while he himself directed the operations from his office. We, in turn, filled him in on our story.

I was dying to know what brought him to Amman and assumed it was a job. The answer was surprising. No, Karim told us, he had not come on a job: he had brought no passenger and wasn't intending to take anyone back. He said that he 'just felt like coming to see us' and was planning to return the following day. I couldn't hold back my question any longer: 'Can we travel with you to Damascus? You know God has sent you.'

Karim nodded his head in silent wonder and amazement. "I will certainly take you back with me to Damascus. Can you be ready by mid morning, tomorrow?"

Of course, we could. The next day, six months – not the expected two weeks – after we had entered Amman, we left it. Not going back home, but northwards to Damascus and Baalbek.

Yet as we set out, sitting in comfort in a most luxurious car driven by my own brother, it was not hard to see God's loving hand on me and my children.

CHAPTER 13

Syria and Beyond

As we drove northwards towards Syria, Karim became increasingly concerned that we would have trouble at the border. Although there was public sympathy for Palestinian refugees, the fact was Arab states were already closing their doors to those fleeing from Palestine. The only identity documents we had was the Palestinian refugee registration forms issued to us in April. At Ramtha, we reached the Jordanian side of the border. At the checkpoint there, the border police asked for passports or identity cards. I offered him all I had. The official looked at the papers with disbelief. 'We can't stop you from leaving' he said in a voice filled with sympathy, 'but if the Syrians refuse you entry, we won't take you back.'

I realised for the first time how vulnerable we were now. We were stateless: we belonged nowhere and no one wanted us. Then a prophecy from Isaiah about Christ came to my mind, 'what he shall open, no one shall shut' and I felt comforted. I knew that God was leading us forward through a door he had opened and that nothing would stand in our way.

I returned to the car – to Karim's visible relief – and we drove across the barren brown emptiness of no man's land to the Syrian checkpoint at Dera. Here again, my prayers were answered. I showed the border guards my letter and telegram from the school and when they saw that our destination was Lebanon, they let us through without even a question. We were going to be some one else's problem.

In Damascus, I had a wonderful reunion with Adib and Halim and their wives and children. They were all very welcoming and loving and we shared news of our family. Over the next few days, my dear brothers bought and paid for every item that the children needed for school: the warm woollen underwear was especially welcome. My time in Damascus turned into a brief, wonderful and much needed holiday. Each day, we were taken to visit famous and interesting places in the ancient city. There were famous places from the book of Acts; 'the street called Straight', the house of Ananias and the part of the city wall where Paul was let down in a basket to escape imprisonment and possibly death at the hands of the Jews in Damascus. There was the great Ommayid mosque of Damascus with its columns and minarets. The children's favourite was none of these; it was the endless narrow streets and alleyways of the ancient souks. Each part of the souk specialised in one specific type of merchandise so there was the gold souk, the sandals souk, the toy souk and even one that specialised in mouth-watering crystallised fruit. My own favourites were those stalls and bazaars that sold the world-renowned, glittering silk and silver thread embroidered fabrics.

All too quickly, the time spent in Damascus came to an end. One memorable visit was from Pauline Stammers of the British Syrian Mission, who introduced herself to us and showed us round the mission school in the old Bab Tuma part of Damascus. Pauline also offered to take us in her car to the bus station to catch the coach to Baalbek.

Once more, it was time for goodbyes. I was torn by emotions. Perhaps most of all, I felt joyful and excited. I knew that while we may have looked sallow-faced and poorly dressed, a new and bright future awaited us. That hope strengthened my resolve and put a new spring in my step. I was also extraordinarily grateful to my brothers and their families for all their help. Yet nagging away beneath the joy and the gratitude was the deep throbbing ache of having to leave a daughter behind, even if it was with my beloved and trusted brothers.

As we stacked our suitcases and bags in Pauline's car and then hugged and kissed everyone goodbye, tears ran down my cheeks. We got into the car and I swallowed as I realised that there were just four of us. I stared resolutely ahead as we pulled away, not daring to trust myself to look back at the small group who we left behind, lest I glimpse Huda.

At the bus station, we left the car and took the bus for Lebanon. The bus wound its way westwards out of Damascus along the banks of the River Barada and then began to climb up the flanks of the Anti-Lebanon range of mountains. Soon as the temperature dropped, brown rocky mountains stretched either side of us and to the south the great mass of Mount Hermon, (*Jebel esh Sheikh* in Arabic) emerged from the haze. Increasingly the dry terrain was wild, treeless and strewn with rocks and boulders. The road turned into a winding and narrow mountain pass and soon we were at the Lebanese border.

The bus rolled on down the winding road and suddenly, as we emerged from the narrow pass, an amazing panorama became visible. Stretched out some hundreds of feet below us was a vast, smooth and flat valley carpeted with rectangular fields of varying shades of green and yellow. It was my first and unforgettable glimpse of the Bekaa, the great fertile inland valley of Lebanon that lies between the ranges of the Anti–Lebanon and Mount Lebanon.

At the Syrian border, the guard did not check anyone's papers or passports, but merely walked along the side of the bus looking at the passengers through the windows before waving the driver on. At the Lebanese border, I was asked where we were going. 'Baalbek' I said 'to the English School' and began fumbling for the school letter. Yet the officer had already moved on to the next passenger. With a final prayer of thanks to the Lord, I settled back in my seat to relax the rest of the way.

By now the girls were getting restless with excitement and apprehension. 'Are we nearly there?' they kept asking. A red juicy apple for each soon helped them to settle down again. Yet my heart and thoughts were constantly with Huda in Damascus. How much did she cry? How did she cope? As I thought of her, I felt the tears streaming down my face. I wondered whether I was going to manage.

By the time the tears had cleared, I looked out of the window to see that we had already left the slopes behind us and were on the level ground of the Bekaa valley. So we came to a junction and instead of proceeding westwards over the looming heights of the Mount Lebanon range we turned north onto the Baalbek road.

After another hour's driving northwards on the increasingly brown plain of the Bekaa, the bus driver stopped at the beginning of a town. We had reached Baalbek and the school. Our luggage was unloaded and I turned to the enormous green gates with the metal ring knocker. I glanced at my three daughters, thin and pale faced, and hesitated, feeling my heart thumping against my ribs. Then, lifting the ring, I knocked firmly on the door.

The teacher who opened the door greeted us with a friendly smile and led us to the main building. We had been expected. As we walked from the main gate to the main door, I saw flowerbeds, concrete paths, flowering shrubs, trees and a small raised pond with a fountain in the middle. I had the feeling of an oasis surrounded by buildings.

We were ushered into the lounge to meet Miss Button and all my deep-rooted dislikes of British missionaries came back to unnerve me. The lady who came to meet us was smartly dressed, of average to small build and her chestnut hair was neatly brushed back and gathered into a small bun at the nape of her neck. Her bearing, severe expression and the fact that there was not a hair out of place, confirmed that she was the school principal.

For the briefest of moments, a smile melted the stern expression on her face.

'I hope you and the girls had a comfortable journey and are not too tired,' she said.

Her accent was not British! The tension that had been building up inside me relaxed. Miss Freda Button, it emerged, was Australian. Tea and some biscuits were brought in; both more than welcome after our four hour long journey.

After refreshments, we were taken upstairs to the main dormitory where my girls were to have their sleeping accommodation. It was a large rectangular room with windows on two sides. The windows along the long axis of the room overlooked the front yard and gardens through which we had passed. The window on at the other, narrower end of the room showed a very different vista. I looked out, amazed to see six enormous stone columns rising into the sky and linked at the top by a vast crossbeam covered in intricate carvings. It was my first glimpse of the vast and spectacular Roman ruins of Baalbek. The six pillars were all that remained of the temple of Jupiter after the ravages of severe weather, earthquakes and wars had brought down all the other columns.

I dragged my attention back to the room where Miss Button was explaining where my daughters would be sleeping. I realised that there was something very odd about the room. There were no beds, only mattresses on the floor, eight on each side and each neatly folded back on itself.

'When the girls come up to bed,' continued Miss Button, 'they open the mattresses up to sleep in and similarly fold them back in the morning. The girls are used to sleeping on the floor: that's what they do in their own homes.' How ironic, I thought, I had moaned to God about sleeping on the floor in Amman, and now here we were at boarding school and my daughters were still going to have to sleep on the floor.

We moved on to my sleeping accommodation. This was in one of the outer buildings in a small room shared with the cook, Saidie! Disappointed, I lifted my heart to the Lord in a quick prayer for patience and the acceptance of my situation in good grace. I also prayed for wisdom as I faced the next few days, for understanding what my duties entailed and for the strength to accomplish them to the best of my ability.

That first day I was told something else that I hadn't expected and something that came as another sharp blow. It was that because I was a member of staff, during term time, I had to sever my relationship with my daughters as they were with the other girls. They could risk no favouritism.

God had answered our prayer in getting us here but I realised that regular prayer was going to be needed to keep us here.

CHAPTER 14

Beginning at Baalbek

I soon found that I was responsible for almost every aspect of the students' lives, apart from their studies. I had lists of house duties to write out, the laundry to organise, bedtime and waking up time duties to be supervised and the sick to be cared for. They were vital and demanding tasks yet somehow I did them. I became known to the children as 'Sitt Wadeah', Miss Wadeah in English.

On top of these responsibilities, I had other duties. I was also in charge of organising the food and the kitchen, so I had to order the weekly provisions and plan menus with the cook and because the staff and the girls ate different meals that meant planning two separate menus a day. I also had to find and supervise a cleaning woman to do the housework. There were so many new things to learn and remember. At first, too I frequently found Lebanese Arabic difficult to follow and I misunderstood some idiomatic expressions. For a long time too, the Lebanese currency also confused me.

I was also responsible for the washing arrangements. Wardeh, a Palestinian woman from the Wavell refugee camp just outside Baalbek, was hired for two days a week to do the washing and ironing for the staff. We had a large washroom in the outer buildings that boasted a large copper vessel for heating water, a stone sink with a coldwater tap above it, a big aluminium basin and a number of low wooden stools and buckets. Here on Saturdays, the girls who were old enough did their own washing. Wardeh washed the clothes of those who were too young to do it themselves. On Friday and Saturday nights, the washroom doubled up as a common bathroom. Depending on their age, four or five girls would have their baths together. Each would fill a bucket with hot water from the copper vessel, use one of the stools to sit on and proceed to wash herself. Fortunately, I had to bath the little ones myself and that way I was able to make sure that Ibtisam and Afaf were properly bathed: Siham was old enough to cope on her own.

As the days grew shorter, it wasn't long before I found I had another duty. I had to order tons of logs for heating in the winter months. High, and exposed to cold winds blowing down from the mountains to the east and the west, Baalbek could be bitterly cold and every room, except the bedrooms, had an iron stove with a metal chimney. When the temperature dropped, logs would be expertly arranged in the stoves and a fire lit which quickly warmed up the room. Each morning before school started, one girl from each class would come to the woodshed to collect the daily consignment of logs. Organising that too, was my responsibility.

Those early months in Baalbek were hard. I found the town very different from sophisticated Haifa. Ancient Baalbek may have once been a splendid centre of Roman civilisation but in the late 1940s it was simply a poor rural market town situated a long way from anywhere else. Life at the school itself was exceedingly basic, there was electricity but not in the classrooms in the outer buildings. Evening study time and prep were held in two of these classrooms, a shorter prep for the younger girls and a longer one for the older pupils. Suspended from the centre of each ceiling were two mantle-light lamps and, by producing a jet of kerosene spray into the small fragile lace-like sack which when lighted became incandescent and gave a brilliant light.

Every morning and evening, I had to help the little ones with making their beds and folding up their mattresses. There were other similar practices that seemed archaic as well as time-consuming. My natural instinct and inclination was to change and improve the facilities in the boarding house as fast as possible. But then I have to remind myself of the great upheaval the school must have undergone in moving to Baalbek. With patience and time I was sure the school would become all I hoped it would be.

Soon the unfamiliar chillness of the winter became an added burden. By late November, snow had covered the mountaintops either side of the Bekaa valley and the regular winter storms brought heavy snowfalls to Baalbek itself and the wood stoves became essential.

My three older daughters settled down quickly and very well at the school. Academically, it was a struggle to begin with. There had been too many interruptions and disruptions in their lives in the last few months, and the Lebanese curriculum was totally different from the British one of Palestine.

In the midst of all my activities, I could never forget my daughter who I had left over the mountains in Damascus. One day, I had a telephone call from my brother Adib to say that Huda was not very well; would I go over for a couple of days?

Miss Button did not object and Friday afternoon saw me on my way to Damascus, willing the bus to grow wings and fly me to my daughter as fast as could be. I will never forget the joy of seeing her again, I enveloped her with my arms and couldn't let go. Her health was not as bad as I had feared; she'd just had a bad cold and was now getting over it. Apart from that, she was looking well and had a lovely dress on. My brothers, sisters-in-law, nephews and nieces had all seen to it she lacked nothing and had showered love and care on her. Yet I was not reassured; that night Huda slept in my bed but was very restless. Half awake, her hand kept going over my face, feeling it in the dark and saying, 'Mama? Mama?' 'Yes darling, I'm here,' I would answer, 'go to sleep." She did this three or four times during the night. The two days in Damascus went by all too quickly and as I prepared to leave, I explained to Huda as best as I could, the need for me to return to work so that, one day soon, she could come to school and be with us all. I found leaving her this second time even harder than the first. Suddenly, a firm determination welled up inside me to find a way to have Huda with me again. I prayed to God from the depths of my aching soul that he would soften the principal's heart and let my daughter join us soon. That evening, after I had arrived back at the school, I managed to have a few minutes together with my three daughters in my room to discuss and pray about the situation. I was soon crying.

A few days later, Miss Button called me to her office. Unknown to us, she had happened to go past my room that night and, through the slightly open door, had observed both the family meeting and the tears. She suggested bringing Huda over to join me, although she warned, it was to be 'on a trial basis only'. 'Thank you, thank you very much' was all I could say. I was overwhelmed by the kindness of this woman who seemed to sense our needs and problems at every turn in our life. We discussed the details, including Huda's sleeping accommodation; to begin with, she would have to share my room. Visualising the small room that I shared with the cook, I didn't dare ask how it would be possible. Yet I felt sure that, as God had so speedily answered my prayers, he would take care of the details.

When the wonderful news reached Damascus, the whole family rejoiced with me. They had all become so attached to Huda, especially my three sisters-in-law, Selma, Linda and Latifeh, that they found it hard to let her go. Fouad, one of my nephews had developed a close friendship with my little daughter, and it was he who brought her to Baalbek. Fouad carried Huda's little suitcase with one hand and held her hand with the other as she skipped along beside him, a very happy little girl going to join her mother and sisters. Overjoyed at seeing her sisters, and me, Huda was nevertheless dismayed at the news that Fouad's visit to Baalbek was only a short one and that he had to return to Damascus the same day.

Although Huda settled quickly and happily into the school

routine, she was slightly disoriented and confused to start with. I opened her little suitcase to put her clothes in the chest of drawers in the room but as soon as I placed one set of underwear in, she would grab them out of the drawer and put them firmly back in the suitcase. 'They're mine, they're mine,' she kept saying. A number of times, too, in those early days in Baalbek, she would call me 'Auntie'. Yet, overall, there were no ill effects in Huda's life, psychological or otherwise, as a result of that short period of separation. She was to be become a wise and loving mother herself and eventually, a proud grandmother as well.

With Huda now present with us, other issues became important. The most pressing of these was school and boarding fees. It was all too obvious that what I earned would not even pay for two girls, let alone four at school. Talking the matter over with Miss Button, I even suggested that in order to pay for my daughters, I might have to resign my job at the school and find a better paid one. This was not an idle comment: there was a very strong possibility of nursing work with the newly established UNWRA (United Nations Welfare and Relief Agency) who were now running the Wavell refugee camp outside Baalbek and they paid very well. Miss Button though, would not hear of it. 'Wadeah, God sent you to *us*' she said, 'not to the refugee camp.' Yet, as ever, Miss Button's faith didn't stop her from taking practical action to try and find a way to cover the deficit we were incurring. All refugee children registered at Wavell Camp and who were receiving rations – flour, sugar and dried milk – were entitled to free education. On investigation it emerged that, as refugees, my four daughters could be registered with the UN. I did this and from then on, after school every Friday, one of my daughters would go with Wardeh, our washing woman, to the camp, sign the book and be given the rations, which were then passed on to the grateful Wardeh! The UN authorities then paid the education fees for the school. I rejoiced in the fact that God did not make us a burden on the school.

My main worry was not the girls' education, but their health. They were seriously undernourished and not eating the right kind of foods. Lebanese country food, especially in winter, was very strange to our palates. No fresh vegetables were available, only dried ones which, when cooked, turned leathery and tough. Breakfast was the worst. It was based on *kishk* (dried yoghurt) reconstituted with water and boiled to form a thickish broth that was served steaming hot. It was an ideal winter breakfast in the snowy months: there was just one problem; it smelt, and tasted, horrible. On one occasion, Ibtisam and Afaf just sat there looking at their bowl of hot *kishk* and refused to touch it. It made them feel sick, they said: they couldn't eat it. By now, all the other girls had finished their breakfast and left the dining room. Embarrassed by my daughters obstinacy and disobedience I became furious. I made them carry their bowls, go outside, and stand in the snow until they finished it.

Looking back on my action, I think that perhaps I over-reacted and that wasn't the only occasion. But what drove such actions was the constant fear I had that some act of misbehaviour would result in us losing our place at the school. God had provided for us both a home and a source of education for my daughters in the school. The Wavell refugee camp nearby was a reminder of how fortunate we now were. I found out later many years later that my fear was not unique; Ibtisam was in constant dread lest Huda would misbehave in some way and would be sent back to Damascus. So if her sister cried, Ibtisam would run to her and pacify her in any way she knew; by giving her sweets, telling her a story or just by playing with her. We were all very conscious of our precarious situation yet I feel that our worries were groundless: we had not appreciated the fact that God who provided this haven for us in the first place was able to keep us there.

CHAPTER 15

Baalbek Years

Yet for all the many answers to prayer, life during that first year at the school was hard. My position as matron, nurse and housekeeper was difficult and the additional demands of being a mother to four daughters stretched me even further. Huda, who was still not yet four, attended school only in the morning: something that caused problems in the afternoons. Refusing to rest, or to play alone in her room, she would often be heard crying and calling 'Mama!', 'Auntie!', 'Miss!', 'Sitt Wadeah!' any name that she felt would produce a response. But the Lord gave me wisdom, strength, and grace in the eyes of my employers. The last was something that was important because I was not the easiest person to employ; I could never keep quiet about things that I considered wrong or that needed improvement. I would either go to those in authority or take my request to the Lord directly. One day, Tahia, one of the new members of staff, said to me, with a twinkle in her eye 'you're not afraid of the missionaries, Sitt Wadeah?' 'No,' I replied. 'Only of God.'

One example of my attitude occurred in the matter of the beds. The end of each term brought new duties; all the clothes had to be checked and counted before the girls were picked up by their parents for the holidays. One end of term duty that I found especially burdensome was that of piling all the mattresses in the bedrooms into one corner, an exhausting task even with the help of some of the older girls. On one occasion, as I was still on my knees in the middle of the dormitory, I lifted my arms in prayer and prayed aloud for

God to provide extra funds for the mission to buy beds for the girls. A few moments later, Leila, one of the girls who was with me, whispered to me 'Sitt Wadeah, Miss Button has just gone along the corridor and saw you praying!'

Whether it was the prayer or the fact that it was overheard, I do not know but within two months, some money was sent to the school as a gift and beds were bought for all the girls.

With time, in some cases encouraged by my promptings, other improvements were made to the school. Flushing cisterns appeared above the toilets and basins with running water were put in the girls' washroom! Mind you, it was still cold water and in winter, the pipes often froze and burst.

On one issue, my outspoken manner resulted in a major confrontation with Miss Button, which could have cost me my job. Thankfully, it didn't and instead, cemented a deep friendship between us. The issue arose because of the practice of having separate bathrooms and toilets for missionaries and local staff. After keeping silent for a long time, I finally spoke out openly and firmly on this matter. I argued that to behave in this way showed lack of love and sensitivity towards those Christian brothers and sisters who were our colleagues. Miss Button was very hurt and reduced to tears. Initially, she could not see anything wrong: 'That's how it was in Ain Zhalta,' she said 'why should it change now?' As she spoke, I realised that I could do no more: only God could change attitudes of the heart. So said no more and simply got on with my duties.

I don't know the details of what happened next but the following month I found two carpenters busy at work upstairs in the main building putting up partitions at either end of the long corridor, converting the space into what looked like two small rooms. One room I knew about: there were plans to create a clinic where girls could come and see me if they were feeling ill or needed some medication. When it was finished, the clinic was very attractive and professional. The surprise was at the other end of the corridor, where a similar partition was being constructed resulting in a spacious airy and light room which opened on to the balcony. As I stood there admiring it, Miss Button came up and said simply. 'Wadeah, this is your room. Congratulations!' I was so overwhelmed with gratitude for the kindness I had been shown that I could say nothing.

My few belongings and those of my young daughter were soon transferred to the new room in the main building. For the first time since we had left our home in Haifa, I no longer felt a refugee! When Miss Button came to see if everything was all right, she sat on the edge of the bed and looked round the pleasant and cosy room opening on to the balcony and said 'My father would have been very happy to see his money used for this.'

Unknown to anyone, she had used her own money – a small legacy her father had left her before he died – to build those two rooms. She turned to me. 'Do you mind if we pray to thank God and dedicate this room to His glory and to the memory of my father?'

Of course, I didn't mind and our prayers flowed out not only for that room, but also for the whole work and purpose of the school. Was the room Miss Button's peace offering to me to show there were no permanent hard feelings? I don't know, but I do know that the love of God was truly in that woman's life.

As the summer came, the question of holidays came up. It was one thing living at the school during term time but the staff at Mission Headquarters thought it wouldn't be suitable for the girls and me to stay there during the holidays. At the two-week long Christmas and Easter vacations, my brothers had put us all up in Damascus. Yet it was not a satisfactory solution. Although the house was a large one, there were already three families living in it and after the Easter holidays I resolved that we would not, under any circumstances, burden them again.

On our return to school for the summer term, I explained

the situation to Miss Button and suggested that I would rent accommodation outside the school so we would have somewhere to stay during our holidays too. She nodded her head and told me to wait a little and pray about it. No doubt she did pray, but with Miss Button, prayer went hand-in-hand with action. We later found out that at the next executive meeting of mission personnel, she had asked that we be allowed to use school premises during vacation time. There was strong opposition to this suggestion, but not enough to dissuade this resolute lady from her purpose. She stood up, faced the council members and said 'if the Musallam family are not given a home during their holidays I will resign.' Immediately, another missionary, Iris Nash, stood up in her support. That was enough for Miss Fitzpatrick, the chair of the committee. After a short discussion, there was general consent that we be allowed to stay all year round.

So for our summer vacation that year we stayed in the school. Over the years that followed that mission house was not just a beautiful and peaceful oasis for many visiting missionaries and visiting preachers, it was also our own very dear home.

The three months long summer holidays turned out to be as busy as the term time. A great deal of the food the school consumed in winter was prepared during the summer months. So amid the dry dusty summer heat of the Bekaa we turned tomatoes into gallons of puree, plums and apricots into jams, pumpkins and ginger into preserve. We filled sacks with dried apricots, apple rings, prunes and raisins. We threaded pounds and pounds of okra (ladies fingers) and aubergines on strings and let them dry in the sun. Wheat and pulses were ordered and stored. The wheat had to be milled to make flour and cracked into *burghul* for various local traditional dishes. At home as a child, I had helped my mother in some similar food preparations but not to the same extent. Here too, there were unfamiliar varieties and quantities. Once again, God's strength, grace and wisdom supported me and slowly I learnt all these lessons.

In this area as well, changes were introduced over the years. It became increasingly economical to buy many of these products ready prepared from wholesalers rather than make them ourselves. Ever the traditionalist, Miss Button took some convincing, but was finally won over.

Although my daughters had recovered from the hard months in Amman, they were still physically weak and tended to succumb easily to illnesses and ailments. Ibtisam seemed to cough constantly and the medicines prescribed her by the local doctor had little effect. Three years running, Huda developed a skin infection in spring that lasted throughout the summer. Both daughters needed to see specialist doctors but we could not afford their fees. In his mercy, God intervened.

Baalbek was (and still is) a mainly Moslem town and there were only a limited number of Christians. So although there were Maronite and Roman Catholic churches, there was no Protestant church. Sunday morning services were held in our school hall which doubled as chapel and were open to anyone who wished to attend from the town. On one particular Sunday, the visiting preacher was a well-known Egyptian pastor, Fahmi Hannawi. At the end of the service, I went over to Mr. Hannawi and asked him if he had experience in healing. He told me that all I needed was faith in the word of God. I remembered the words in James' epistle 'Is anyone among you sick? Let him call for the elders of the church, and let them pray over him, anointing him with oil in the name of the Lord'[9].

An Armenian schoolgirl – Mary Tournekian – also came forward with my daughters. Mary had a rheumatic heart and was very ill indeed. Mr. Hannawi asked the three girls if they believed Jesus could heal them. They answered that they did and Mr. Hannawi prayed for them and anointed them with oil. The next morning, as I helped Huda to get dressed I

[9] James 5.14

noticed that the spots on her body had all dried up. Ibtisam came running to me and said, 'Look. Mama the cough has gone; it isn't there anymore!' I thanked God for his mercy on us and for his healing of my daughters. Later that day, Mary came to me and asked shyly, 'Sitt Wadeah, how would I know that I've been healed too?' As best as I could, I assured Mary that God had healed her even though we couldn't see the result immediately. In fact, Mary recovered, grew up into a strong and healthy young woman, got married and had a family. Her heart weakness had completely disappeared.

Slowly, we began to be at home in Baalbek. We came to know the vast ruins well and spent many happy hours as a family walking amongst the fallen and disjointed columns and tumbled mighty blocks of stone. We came to know the local people and almost to be accepted as locals ourselves. We were Palestinians but we were also Christians in a strong Muslim community.

We spent the holidays together in Baalbek. Very often, Miss Button would join us for part of her holiday, as if she was one of the family. We would go for day outings to some beauty spot, take our picnic food with us and just enjoy the hot summer's day lazing in the country or walking in the woods. A particularly popular place was Ras el Ain; 'the head of the spring', where we could actually see the water bubbling up out of the ground to form a pool of clear water which fed into the stream. With its water, green meadows and shady trees, Ras el Ain made an ideal place for a day's outing.

So the years passed. Dry, parching summers would give way to frozen winters when heavy snowfalls turned everything white and the crisp icy winds froze every drop of water and moisture in its path. And the winters would, in turn, yield to the gentle thaws of spring.

I followed the news of Palestine from a distance. Many of our family had stayed behind and lived under Israeli occupation. My mother now lived in Nazareth and my brother Emile had begun to develop the writing career that was to make him famous. But there was no sign of a solution that would allow those of us outside the country to return. As the years passed, I began to adjust more and more to the idea that I would never go back to Haifa. For better or worse, Lebanon was now our home.

The girls grew. In 1951 Siham moved down to Beirut to continue her schooling at the Beirut branch of the mission school, returning to us for holidays. Those days were always happy ones as we enjoyed being a family without the constraints and pressures of school rules and other people. At Christmas and Easter, there were visits to Damascus to my brothers to celebrate the feast days together. As a Middle Easterner, family ties are important and precious to us. I did my best to keep in touch.

In the early fifties Freda Button left us moving down to Beirut to set up a Teacher Training department for the mission.

In 1955, after I had had seven hard, but fulfilling, years in Baalbek, things changed. It became apparent that the school was gradually winding down its boarding department and that my services would soon not be needed. I never really found out why this happened, whether it was the lack of new students or just a decision from the mission directors to concentrate on the main school in Beirut. In my heart, I knew that the time had come for us to move on. It was a disturbing time. Having known homelessness and extreme poverty, I had come to treasure what the school had offered me. I was now nearly fifty and had no desire at all to return to uncertainty; I wanted to cling on to the world that I knew. I was suddenly afraid of the world outside the school walls: it was totally foreign to me and I felt that I had no protection or guidance whatsoever.

In the midst of all this uncertainty, God's word was a constant in my life. The day that I realised I was going to have to leave Baalbek, my Bible reading was from the first chapter of Deuteronomy and as I read verse 6, 'The Lord

God said to us at Horeb, 'you have stayed long enough at this mountain,' it was as if God was speaking directly to me and my children. I realised that I had made myself too comfortable in Baalbek. Encouraged and given a new determination, I turned my face to whatever the future might hold for us. I was certain that the God who had led us thus far would not abandon us.

CHAPTER 16

Beirut

I had to leave the school but where to go? The obvious answer was Beirut. By now, my three brothers who had been in Damascus had moved to Beirut with their families.

The mid fifties was start of the golden age of Beirut. It was then still a small and charming capital city, largely confined to a promontory that jutted into the blue Mediterranean and overlooked by the wooded foothills and small red roofed villages of Mount Lebanon. Yet Beirut was not just a beautiful setting; Lebanon's capital was the undisputed intellectual and financial centre of the Middle East, the meeting point between the Arab world and the West and the place where the Arabs of the Gulf States, newly enriched by oil, came for shopping and pleasures of any kind. Beirut overflowed with money, ideas and dreams.

The headland of Ras Beirut was the fashionable and wealthy part of the city. It was fringed by the seaside promenade of the Corniche, a wide dual carriageway whose pavements were lined with palm trees, restaurants and cafes to suit every taste. Behind the Corniche, stood the most elegant and luxurious apartment buildings you could find anywhere in the Middle East where outside glittering marbled entrances, chauffeurs waited by large polished cars.

Beirut was an extraordinarily cosmopolitan city; a mixture of East and West, of Christian and Muslim and a place where English, French and Arabic could be heard, sometimes in the same sentence. The focus of the city's cultural and intellectual life was the American University of Beirut, which had been founded nearly a hundred years earlier by missionaries but which had, sadly, lost any Christian vision long ago. The university had a vast, and spectacularly beautiful, campus that sloped down to the sea where it had its own private beach. Then, and for many years later, AUB was of such a high academic standing that it ranked with some of the finest educational institutions in the United States. Linked to AUB was the American University Hospital (AUH), indisputably the finest hospital in the Middle East at the time and one that drew both medical students and patients from all over the world.

One of my nieces worked as a lab technician at AUH and seeing an advertisement for midwives, immediately contacted me. Taking a short leave from the school, I went down to Beirut to stay with my brother Adib who lived the closest to the university. Over the next few days, I applied for the post of midwife, was interviewed and got the job. It was the beginning of June, just one month before the school closed for summer.

I started work at AUH with some concerns. The work involved night duties that I felt were going to place an extra strain on me and the family once we set up home in Beirut. My main worry was that it had been a long time since I worked in a hospital and most of my previous midwifery practice and experience had been done on a private basis in the home. Despite my determined efforts, it became clear over the next month that I was out of touch with the modern hospital routines and procedures practised in AUH. In the nearly thirty years since I had begun my training, methods and techniques in the delivery rooms had moved on and changed remarkably. I felt lost and could not cope. My vulnerability was not helped by the presence of many younger nursing staff, mainly Armenians, who were more up to date with the hospital requirements. They had little time for me and when one of those nurses started taking over my duties without consulting me and physically pushing me out of the way, I decided to give in my notice.

The news that I had given up my job was not well received and brought me a lot of criticism and blame, particularly from my brothers and their families. Their concern was understandable: as 'family' they felt responsible for me and knew that, without a job, they would have to support the girls and me. Once, when I assured one of my nieces of God's care for me, she turned round and said to me 'God is a figment of your imagination.'

Like some unwanted animal, I left Beirut and crept back to my children and the only home we had; the school in Baalbek. I felt defeated and afraid. My time was running out and we would soon have to leave and venture out into the world. The slim chance of any reprieve vanished when it was confirmed that the boarding department of the school was definitely closing down and that I wouldn't be needed the following September.

One small ray of hope was that Siham had just completed her teacher's training and had been taken on the staff of the Lebanese Evangelical School for Girls (LESG) in Beirut to start teaching in September. But that raised other issues; she would need a place to live. I knew I had to move on, I continued to trust in the God who had never abandoned either my family or me. I knew I could leave the unknown and all the details of the future in God's hands.

God gave me precious moments of reassurance at that testing time. One hot day, as I walked through the centre of Baalbek I found myself gazing through the shop windows at the many things we would need to set up home from scratch. As I did, I found myself, perhaps for the first time, yearning for the home and all our possessions that we had lost in Haifa. I was struck by the enormity of the task ahead of us as a family. We had absolutely nothing; how could we find the money for all our needs? As I pondered these thoughts, I heard a voice behind me suddenly say 'I'm rich, very rich', repeating the phrase three times. I turned round to see who had spoken the words, only to find it was a small schoolboy

– no more than six years old – apparently repeating some line that he had learnt at school. But I had heard God speak to me in his words and there in the street, I lifted my heart to the Lord and thanked him for reminding me of his riches.

In July, I visited Beirut and found a small third floor flat within walking distance of the school that Siham was going to teach at and rented it. My brother Halim paid the rent for the first six months in advance. I returned to Baalbek and a couple of weeks later, we gathered together the few belongings we had and left the place that had been our much loved home for the last seven years.

The apartment in Beirut was small but adequate for our immediate needs, especially as we had hardly any furniture. The best thing about the flat was its proximity to LESG where Siham would teach and the other three girls would go to study. By now, Ibtisam was in her last year of primary school and had to pass the government exam, while Afaf and Huda were respectively one and two years behind her.

The early weeks in our simple home were very happy and exciting. Although the room in the Baalbek school had been welcome, it had always been the school's and never, in any real sense, ours. Now though we had our own apartment and in a way that perhaps, we had never had before, we seemed to be a real family. We had time for one another to talk, to share our dreams and our hopes. Slowly, the bare flat became a comfortable home.

The sophistication and bustle of Beirut excited the girls and they looked forward to our shopping trips 'down town' to buy those few essentials we could afford. The school uniforms were the highest priority on our shopping list. The girls needed two sets, one for the summer and one for winter. They would start the autumn term in the summer uniform, switching to the winter one when the weather broke.

Despite all this activity, I could not forget the increasingly urgent need to find some employment with a regular income in order for us to survive. There were large payments to be made for school fees and uniforms and in a few months, there would be rent to be paid. The headmistress of the girls' school, Hazel St. John, who knew our situation from Miss Button, offered me some work for a few weeks. LESG were making new covers for chairs and settees in the different lounges at the school and I helped with the sewing. Yet that soon ended and worry began to invade my life; anxious days merged into sleepless nights. I tried to get some employment with 'Point Four', an American Organisation – started by President Eisenhower – very active in children's education and social welfare working in developing countries. But I was unsuccessful. My concern mounted; we were running out of money.

Finally, one day I asked myself where my trust in God had gone. Could I have really forgotten how he had led us from Amman to Lebanon, providing all our needs along the way and given us a home in Baalbek for the last seven years? Had he not now given me a helper in my daughter who was supporting the whole family? Such thoughts lifted my spirits but then the concerns crept back. Despite the encouragement and support of my daughters, learning to live by faith, one day at a time, was not easy.

Soon it was early October and time for the schools to open. I couldn't resist standing on the balcony that first morning to watch my four daughters walk to school; Siham starting her first day of work and the three younger ones dressed in their smart new school uniforms. Pride and joy filled my heart. They turned a corner and I went back into the house.

Just then, the doorbell rang. I was not expecting any callers, and certainly none at that early hour. I opened the door to find David Tleel there. David was the treasurer and General Secretary of the Mission in Beirut at the Head Office and I had known both David and his sister Katy, years before in Haifa. Glad to have a visitor, I welcomed David into the apartment.

David explained that he had come to ask if I would teach

Arabic to a Mr and Mrs Joyce, an American missionary couple. I hesitated; I had never done any teaching before and Arabic is a complex language. However, when David explained the new method of teaching the spoken language and showed me the books they would be using, it sounded both very interesting and something that I felt I could do very well. He arranged for me to meet the Joyces the following day: that meeting was a success and I made arrangements with them to go to their house on a regular basis to teach them.

So, unexpectedly, began my second career. The Joyces were to be the first of many missionaries who were to be taught and helped with their Arabic by me over the next twelve years. Wonderfully, our immediate needs were met and our future was secure. I had an apartment, a rewarding job, one daughter with a job and three other daughters in one of the best schools in Beirut. God had been faithful to me!

As I thought about God's faithfulness, I suddenly remembered my childhood vow, the promise I had made so long ago to offer myself as a sacrifice to God. Now, faced with further evidence of his kindness to me I realised that I needed to know how to repay God. I found the answer in the Bible. At the start of the twelfth chapter of his letter to the Romans, Paul had written this: 'I appeal to you therefore, brothers, by the mercies of God, to present your bodies as a living sacrifice, holy and acceptable to God, which is your spiritual worship.' And in the Letter to the Hebrews there was a similar challenge: 'through Jesus, therefore, let us continually offer to God a sacrifice of praise...for with such sacrifices God is pleased.'[10] I realised that God did not want me to respond to his love to me with a single action; he wanted my entire life, whether in worship or in my work, to be holy and pleasing to him. I made a life-long commitment to a life of holiness and to trying to please God in all I did.

[10]Hebrews 13.15

Sometime after I had settled into my new routine of teaching, my brother Halim paid me a visit with some surprising news: mother was leaving Israel and coming to live in Beirut. After leaving Haifa in April 1948, she had gone to live with my sister and her family in Nazareth. She had eventually been able to reclaim her home in Haifa back from the Israeli government who had confiscated all abandoned or empty houses, and had returned there. My sister, now widowed with four daughters and a son, had moved in with her. Now very elderly, mother wanted to be with us in Beirut.

I looked at Halim, 'But where would mother live in Beirut?'

Even before he uttered a word, the expression on his face told me the answer: my brothers expected me to look after her. In the end, I agreed to have her although we both knew how very difficult and impractical it would be. She was in her eighties and so heavily built that her legs couldn't properly support her, we were on the third floor, and the building had no lift.

A few weeks later, mother arrived. It was a tearful but happy reunion. Mother looked older and slightly apprehensive, yet that look of determination on her face that I knew so well was still there. Over the next few weeks slowly and painfully she shared with me all that they went through since she and my father left Haifa, particularly father's illness, his final days and his death. Soon she recovered her strength and her usual cheerfulness, becoming very much part of our family and joining in most of our activities. The stairs were no longer a problem nor a hindrance to her going out.

On one memorable occasion, she was even first out of the building. That was the night of March 16th 1956, the night of the earthquake. Lebanon is not particularly prone to earthquakes but they do occur. That evening I was already in bed but not yet asleep and Siham was sitting at the table preparing her schoolwork for the following day. The rest of the household were asleep: mother in her room and Ibtisam, Afaf and Huda in their bedroom. Suddenly, without any warning, the room swayed first to the right and then to the left. There was a second mad swing and the floor seemed to tilt. An intense rumbling noise surrounded us and everything around me, the table, my bed and everything else on the floor, jumped up and down. I had been in a small earthquake in 1941, and I knew instantly what was happening but before I could say a word, Siham began screaming. The other three daughters came running into the room looking utterly scared and bewildered. 'An earthquake,' I said, 'Quickly! Grab a jumper and a dressing gown. Let's go down stairs and get outside.' I was afraid there would be aftershocks or even more quakes and I wanted to be outside in the open space in front of the house.

I suddenly remembered my mother. Going towards her room, I noticed that the front door was open. Mother was already making her way down the stairs heavily and mumbling loudly to herself, 'I'm not going to die under the rubble!'.

I found myself smiling. I found her stick and shawl took them down with me. There seemed to be hundreds of people outside in the square huddled together and speaking in undertones as if afraid that raising their voices might bring another quake. Mostly they were people who had come from the nearby blocks of flats but soon there were others who had came to check on relatives and friends. One of those was my brother Naim who came over quickly to see if we were all right. He then took mother with him and they went for a drive into the countryside! I think it was actually more to calm his own nerves than for her benefit. In fact, we got off lightly: elsewhere in Lebanon 136 people died and 6000 buildings were destroyed.

We soon became settled in the routine of city life. Five of my brothers with their families were now living in Beirut and the Habiby clan was now well represented. There was no shortage of any family activities or celebrations. In 1957, Adib's family organized a delightful twenty-first birthday party for Siham at their home and invited both her colleagues from school and many other friends.

My teaching career was soon well established. Many of my students were mainly from TEAM, a missionary society that worked in the Gulf States. Their new members stopped in Beirut for a year to learn Arabic and then moved on to their various destinations. They were mainly medical people, both doctors and nurses and some, such as Pat and Marion Kennedy and Joann (Eaton) Young became life long friends. They introduced me to Scrabble, a game to which I became addicted. There were many evenings when they appeared on our doorstep with the Scrabble board under one arm and a huge bag of popcorn under the other.

We were in our third year in the flat when I heard that a family of English missionaries, Jack Blockley, his wife and their young daughter were returning to Jordan and vacating a very pleasant ground-floor flat with a small garden. It was just the flat, as the building had never been completed. Curious, I took a look at the flat and when I saw it, I fell in love with it. In my heart, I cried out to God for him to grant us that place for our home. Not only was it a lovely house, I knew it would be ideal for my mother. All the rooms were very spacious; two bedrooms, a dining room, a large lounge, a bathroom and a large kitchen; after where we had lived, it seemed a palace. There was also a small garden with a loquat tree which provided shade for a spacious verandah. I could imagine how, in the hot summer months, mother would sit there on the shaded verandah for most of day doing her fine crochet or needlework lace. Once more, God was gracious to us and our bid to rent the flat was accepted. Before long, we moved in.

Our move coincided with Halim and his family refurbishing their home and replacing their old furniture and carpets with new ones. They gave us what we needed from their old furnishings so that we not only had a new apartment, but we also had it furnished free. The result was that we had a comfortable house that anyone could be proud of. Our house also became the centre for informal family gatherings; it was a place to relax, to exchange news and with mother still in our midst, it seemed just like the old days in Haifa. The garden was an especial blessing as Beirut was desperately short of public parks. Furthermore, it allowed any children who visited to run around and play outside without getting in the way of the grown-ups. We were even able to adopt a stray puppy 'Blacky' who gave the girls great joy in looking after him and he was with us for many years.

Ten years after leaving Haifa with little more than a few bags of clothes we had a wonderful home. How I thanked God for it!

CHAPTER 17

Shadows and Sunlight

For all Lebanon's prosperity and culture, there were many tensions in the society. The country was made up of a number of religious sects, both Christian and Muslim, none of which had an overall majority. The French had bequeathed to Lebanon a constitution that involved power being shared between the different sects so that the President was always a Maronite Christian and the Prime minister a Sunni Muslim and so on. This emphasis on sects meant that every Lebanese was registered as a member of a religious group at birth and that this was written on their identity cards. The result was that people grew up thinking of themselves in terms of their sect, whether they believed in it or not. These religious divisions, and the fact that most Lebanese preferred making money and having a good time to building a nation, meant that the state was remarkably weak. Nevertheless, for much of the 1950s, Lebanon was a peaceful and carefree place.

In the middle of the '50s, turmoil made one of its periodic returns to the Arab world. Under President Nasser, Egypt had begun to take more assertive role in regional affairs, in 1956 Nasser closed the Suez Canal to international shipping, and nationalized it, seizing all private and non-Egyptian assets and ownerships. The result was that in October 1956, Britain and France, assisted by Israel, attacked Egypt. Israel occupied more Arab land and then, a year later, withdrew.

In the early summer of 1958, a shadow fell across the calm of Lebanon when parliament turned down a request by Camille Chamoun, the then President of the Republic, to extend his term of office a further four years. This caused bitterness among the wrangling political parties within the country and highlighted their ongoing deep differences. With the new tensions in the Arab World and the Cold War at its height, what might have been a small internal squabble became an international issue. Many elements from outside Lebanon tried to tip the balance one way or another: these included many Arab states and, if rumour was to be believed, the Russian, British and American intelligence agencies. Suddenly, it seemed as if everybody who had a grudge against Lebanon and its policies was armed and ready to step into the arena. The tendency to take up arms spread sadly to those in the 'Christian' communities in Lebanon. Thankfully, neither in 1958 nor in the later and more catastrophic Civil War that began in 1975, did the Protestant community take any part in the ensuing fighting.

Confusion and fear were widespread in that summer of 1958. Schools closed before the end of the summer term and many families moved out of Beirut up to the mountains and to their summer homes to escape the fighting in the streets of the capital. My daughters and I stayed in our home. Our area was a Muslim district, staunchly against the Chamoun government but very united and stable within itself. We were fairly safe and felt at ease as most of the neighbouring residents knew us. In such a community, a widow with four 'well behaved' daughters would always attract kindly sympathy and protective interest. Nevertheless, the presence of armed men on our street was alarming. One of them, Jumaa, was a Palestinian and was very friendly towards us especially when he found out that we too had come from Palestine. He would always assure me that we had nothing to fear, and that he personally would look after us. I was never sure if the sight of his machine gun slung across his shoulder made me feel more secure in any way! But I, in turn, would often talk to him about the love of God to us through his son Jesus.

On various occasions, I washed and treated this man's wounds and bruises and God gave me peace and courage as I did. One morning, Jumaa was standing outside our front door holding his right hand in front of him. He looked in pain. '*Khalty,*' he said – 'auntie' – a term of respect for an older woman, 'open the door!' As I did, I could see a large black swelling as big as a golf ball in the palm of his right hand. Without thinking, I said 'how did this happen, what did you do to your hand?' He gave me a crooked smile, half pained and half-boasting, and answered, 'I've been beating a man with my gun all night – until he died.'

Every nerve in my body began to vibrate like a plucked string. Jumaa had suddenly become abhorrent and repulsive to me; all I wanted to do was to push this man out of my house. I felt that no power on earth could have made me touch him. Yet somehow, through God's mercy, I recovered sufficiently and was able to look at his hand and do what I could to ease the pain and to make him comfortable. He then told me that the leader of their militia had his headquarters on the ground floor in the building directly opposite our house. We had never noticed or heard anything as all their activities took place at night. They would kidnap men – mostly Christians – off the streets, interrogate them, beat them and, more often than not, kill them and then dump them somewhere outside the city in sacks. Many similar atrocities were committed by both Muslims and also those on the 'Christian' side.

The next time I saw the men hosing down the lobby of the opposite building I understood why. Feeling physically nauseous, I turned and went back into the house. I prayed to God to have pity on the people and to bring an end to all their suffering.

The Civil War ended suddenly when the US, alarmed at the regional consequences should Lebanon become a radical or even communist state, sent a massive fleet to the region and landed troops. Chamoun stepped down and General

Chehab, an army man, was elected as the next president. The crisis was over, the gunmen vanished, the Americans left and peace came back. Yet the issues that had given rise to the Civil War of 1958 were never resolved; they were simply buried as the nation returned to the pursuit of prosperity. They were to flare up again in 1975 and this time the flames were not going to be put out.

Church life was very important to us in those Beirut days. Some of the people who worshipped with us had been leaders of our church in Haifa who had since emigrated to Lebanon. They included my cousin Munir and his wife Kazneh who had been so instrumental to bringing me to faith. After seventeen years of marriage, they had been blessed with a son, Samuel. Wadii Abu Rahmi and his family, old Haifa friends were also there. God again blessed Munir and Wadii's ministry, there were some striking conversions and our church meetings, which were held a few miles from where we lived in the Red Cross hall in Ashrafieh, grew rapidly. Many gifted men and women filled with the Holy Spirit joined the leadership team, including Adley Fam Fanous, a well-known Egyptian preacher who came to live with his family in Lebanon. Music was encouraged in the church: a music director was appointed, a small organ installed and a choir begun. Before long, we had to find a new place for our meetings which had the extra space we needed for the Sunday School and youth groups.

One welcome addition to our church was our dear friend Freda Button who was now the head of the Teacher Training department that she had set up in a new building in the grounds of the Girls' School. Because Christian Arabs tend to use the classical version of Arabic in their worship, most westerners, even if they have mastered the every-day colloquial Arabic, find it hard to participate fully in an Arabic speaking church. Yet Freda's understanding and use of the Arabic language was excellent and adequate for her to be happy attending our church. In those days, we had no car and gladly accepted Freda's offer of transport to church; after the service she would often join us for Sunday lunch at home.

The first seven years we spent in Beirut were a time where my three younger daughters grew through their teenage years. Looking back on them, I feel they were also a time of quiet spiritual nourishment and development through the teaching in our church for all of us. We had seen and experienced God working in our every day lives in some miraculous ways in the past but now was a time of learning more about him and his characteristics. It was also a period when we did what we could to serve God. We had received; now was the time to give.

Soon both Ibtisam and Afaf had finished their school and both went in for secretarial training. Before too long, Afaf started working for an investment company and Ibtisam got a job working in 'Baalbek Studios', a film making organization on the outskirts of Beirut.

Early in 1962, Huda, returning one afternoon from school, found my mother slumped over her needlework in her chair on the verandah. She could neither move nor speak. As soon as I saw her, I realized that she had suffered a major stroke. She did recover slightly, but it became obvious very quickly that she was going to need constant care and nursing. This posed problems because the girls and I were out at work and at school all day. My brother Nakhleh's wife, Afaf, offered to look after her as she was a housewife and did not have to go out to work. At that time they were still living in Syria. So with great sadness, we had to say goodbye to mother as she was taken to Damascus. I managed to visit her twice in the next six months before she died.

Other family news at that time was far more joyful. In the summer of 1963, Siham had been in England taking some summer courses organized by the British Council and had met a young man, Ron Brown. The relationship blossomed and in July 1964 Ronald and Siham were married in Beirut.

The small Anglican Church overlooking the sea was just perfect for their romantic wedding. Among the guests were family members, friends, teaching colleagues of Siham's and her whole class – 30 students, 16-17 year-old girls from Beirut's most elegant society and wealthiest homes. After their honeymoon in Jerusalem and a few days in Beirut, Ron and Siham returned to England to start their married life in London. I was, of course, intensely excited at this first wedding in our family and delighted at having such a son-in-law. Nevertheless, the marriage had repercussions. With Siham leaving us, a substantial part of our household income would disappear. These were lean days for my work too. Most of my Arabic students from TEAM had finished their studies and had moved on. Ibtisam and Afaf were only just starting out on careers and Huda was still at school. Some serious thinking and planning were required. I'm afraid that God was not as involved in these deliberations as he might have been. Yet, even if he was uninvited, God stepped in to my life again. He had already invested a great deal in this family and he wasn't going to leave us stranded.

At the end of one long hot day in August, I was sitting on the verandah in the cool shade of our loquat tree, simply relaxing when I heard in my mind a voice distinctly say, 'how much money would you need?'

I sat up with a jolt. I had not worked out the deficit in our income that would need to be covered: when it came to money matters I was never very well organized. I made a rough calculation and came up with the figure of 400 Lebanese pounds a month which, in those days, was a reasonable income. Two days later, I had a visit from the Reverend Jim Ragland. He was an American who ministered in a Beirut church and who was the principal of the Baptist School in the nearby Mseitbeh suburb. He had a problem: six missionaries had just arrived in Beirut and needed to learn Arabic. Would I have time to teach them? It was not hard to say yes! I had no other commitments at all then. On a piece of paper, Jim jotted down some figures. He turned to me 'Would 700 pounds a month be a sufficient payment?' I had to swallow down the lump that had formed in my throat before I answered 'Yes, thank you'. It wasn't, of course, just Jim Ragland I was thanking; it was God. I was reminded of God's words, in Isaiah 'Before they call I will answer; while they are still speaking I will hear.'[11] How true I had found it! So my teaching of Arabic continued and the new arrangements more than compensated me for the loss of Siham's income.

In October 1965, I had the great joy of becoming a grandmother for the first time when Thea Reem was born to Ron and Siham. The only sadness I had was that I missed being with them for the happy occasion. I had to wait almost nine months before I saw my granddaughter but the occasion on which I saw her made up for the delay.

About this time a young American, Scott McCarty, visited Beirut and came to worship at our church where he met Ibtisam. It was not long before they announced their engagement and Scott's parents came all the way from the States to attend the engagement celebrations of their only son and to meet the family. The marriage of Scott and Ibtisam took place a few months later in February 1966. It was a beautiful and lavish wedding with a great number of guests attending both the church ceremony and the reception. To see two of my daughters already married and to such fine Christian men as Ron and Scott filled my heart with both pride and gratitude to God. I knew it was our heavenly Father who had brought each couple together and I had confidence that he would bless their marriages. After an extensive tour of Europe, Scott and Ibtisam returned to the States, to Georgia where they started their married life on the McCarty Estate.

That summer, with Afaf and Huda, I travelled to England for the first time to visit Ron and Siham and their new baby. We all had a wonderful time together and the highlight of the

[11] Isaiah 65.24

visit was a holiday in Scotland in a hired motor caravan. People often say of some vacation that it was 'the holiday of a lifetime' but in this case, it was indeed true. I had so few holidays of any sort in my life and to be on such a vacation with my beloved family was something that gave me a great joy.

We had arranged for Huda to stay for a year in London with Ron and Siham to study and get some library work experience and so it was only Afaf and I who returned home to Beirut that summer.

The following year, 1967, saw war return to the Middle East. The failure of diplomacy to solve the Palestinian crisis allowed the emergence in the early 60s of Palestinian guerrilla groups, who made periodic attacks across Israel's borders. Tension between Israel and its Arab neighbours increased and feeling threatened by the actions of Egypt's President Nasser, Israel launched a massive attack on the surrounding Arab states in June 1967. In what became known as the Six-Day War, Israel captured the Sinai Peninsula from Egypt, the strategic Golan Heights from Syria and Jerusalem's Old City and the West Bank from Jordan. It was a calamitous defeat for the Arab World and there were now even more Palestinian refugees. Yet, as ever, the war solved nothing; least of all for the Israelis. Among the young Palestinians, the miserable failure of both diplomacy and the Arab leaders meant that the guerrilla warfare option proposed by such groups as the PLO became increasingly attractive. Superficially, Lebanon escaped major damage or loss of territory in the Six-Day War. Yet in the Palestinian camps, there was a new anger and armed Palestinians began to set up bases in those areas of Lebanon that overlooked northern Israel. From one war sprang the seeds of other wars.

Huda returned home at the end of her year in London and found a job as a librarian at the Baptist School. She was very happy there and her work was greatly appreciated. And amid much gratitude to God, I celebrated my sixtieth birthday.

Time passed. Afaf and Huda lived at home with me and I continued with my teaching. At the start of the seventies we said goodbye to our house and moved to a spacious third-floor flat nearby owned by Halim.

Politically, the main events of those years were the rise of the armed and militant Palestinian groups. In order for them to launch attacks, they needed to be in those states which bordered Israel; Lebanon, Syria or Jordan. Despite making loud noises of support for the Palestinian cause, Syria kept a tight control on anything on its territory and allowed little freedom for militant Palestinian organisations. Jordan was, for some time the centre of the Palestinian guerrilla groups and by early 1970, there were a number of such groups based in the refugee camps where they acted outside the control of the Jordanian state. Not only did these guerrilla groups attract Israeli attacks and reprisals but also it was soon apparent that they were becoming a threat to King Hussein and the Jordanian government. Finally, in September 1970, recognising that the future of Jordan was at stake, King Hussein ordered the army to bring these armed groups under control. In a bitter ten-day war, which became known as 'Black September', King Hussein's army crushed the Palestinians. Suppressed in Syria, crushed in Jordan, only Lebanon now remained as a haven for the guerrillas. And after being exiled from Jordan, the Palestine Liberation Organisation set up its military and administrative headquarters in West Beirut. Within the teeming refugee camps, the armed Palestinian organisations grew increasingly powerful and bold. The ill-equipped Lebanese Police and Army increasingly found themselves unable to deal with these powerful groups and the camps became outside the law: 'states within a state'.

Yet despite the gathering storm clouds, these were sunlit years for me. In 1972, Huda was married. Her husband, Ramses, was an Egyptian whom she had met at a Christian summer camp. As Ramses' parents and most of his Egyptian family lived in the United States, they soon moved to join them.

My family seemed to have spread to the ends of earth. Ron and Siham were in London, Scott and Ibtisam were in Lyons, France and Huda and Ramses in California. The apartment seemed empty with just Afaf and me in it.

In autumn 1973, there was another war between the Arabs and Israel. This time it began as the Syrians and the Egyptians launched a surprise attack on the Jewish Holy Day of Yom Kippur. Despite early advances by the Arab armies, the Israelis eventually forced the Syrians and Egyptians back. One good result of this war was that it forced the Israelis and the Egyptians to start negotiating, something that was to lead eventually to the Camp David peace agreement of 1978 between the two countries. Yet neither the war, nor the subsequent settlement, did anything to solve the Palestinian crisis.

In 1975 saw me within sight of my seventieth birthday. But just at a time of life when I might have expected to be able to take things easy and relax, I found myself plunged into the most traumatic and dangerous events of my life.

CHAPTER 18

Another War

In the early 1970s, what had happened in Jordan repeated itself in Lebanon. Palestinian guerrilla groups began to operate as if they ran the country and regularly launched attacks across the border. The Israelis responded by bombing and shelling, frequently injuring or killing Lebanese citizens in the process. When that didn't stop the cross border raids, the Israelis attacked Lebanese targets trying to provoke the Lebanese government into doing what King Hussein had done and crushing the guerrillas. But the Israelis misjudged matters. Lebanon was not Jordan and the Lebanese army was both unwilling and unable to crush what were by now small and powerful armies. Irritated at the threat the Palestinans posed and worried by the Israeli attacks, the Phalangist militias of the Maronite Christians decided that if the government wouldn't – or couldn't – deal with the Palestinian guerrillas, then they would do it for them.

On April 13, 1975, gunmen killed four Phalangists. In retaliation, the Phalangists attacked a bus carrying Palestinian passengers across a Christian neighbourhood of Beirut and killed about twenty-six of the occupants. Samuel, cousin Munir's son, was one of those lined up to be shot. He was saved by one of the gunmen calling out his name with an order to see him. This man was the father of a close school friend at whose house Samuel spent many hours after school. The man took Samuel back home in his own car and delivered him safely to his parents. So began the Lebanese Civil War, a war that was to rumble on for fourteen years, to kill hundreds of thousands and to turn the heart of what had been a once prosperous capital into a pile of ruins. The patterns established on the first day of the war became its hallmark; one atrocity was countered by another of even greater barbarity and no one, women, children or the aged, were immune.

Very soon, the already rather chaotic social framework of Lebanon had collapsed completely. Law and order evaporated, water, electricity and rubbish collection became disrupted and sporadic. Nowhere was safe. Bullets bounced off walls and ricocheted round corners. Mysterious car bombs exploded. People vanished and were never seen again. As stories of abductions and killings became the normal daily news we began to live in fear. Unsurprisingly many, but not all, of the missionaries left and there were some sudden and sad partings.

The longstanding divisions in the city between the Muslim areas (mainly in the west and the south) and the Christian areas (mainly in the east and north) suddenly became very sharply defined. The city became effectively partitioned along what became called the 'Green Line', a zone of empty and increasingly devastated buildings where ferocious exchanges of fire occurred regularly at night and often during the day.

As the war became increasingly seen as one between Palestinian Muslims and Lebanese Christians, we found ourselves in an unpleasant predicament. We belonged to neither party and were in danger from both sides. While the gunmen at the many checkpoints that had sprung up around our home in West Beirut accepted us as Palestinians, our Christian religion made us suspicious in their eyes. The distinction between a Protestant and a Maronite was too subtle for some of the nervous young men who checked papers. And to cross over to the other side of Beirut produced no solution. There our accents betrayed us as hated Palestinians and our claim to be Protestants was viewed with either suspicion or distaste. We felt very vulnerable.

In any event, it soon became very hard to cross the Green Line at all. No taxi would go all the way from one side to another. A Muslim taxi driver would take you to the western edge of the Green Line, then you would have to walk across the deserted stretch between the two sides – praying hard that there were no snipers – before finding a Christian taxi to take you into east Beirut. As our church was on the other side of the Green Line, we didn't go to it; it was too dangerous a journey. No one went out at night. Once night fell, you stayed in your building, trusting that the locked doors would keep out the armed men who cruised the streets. So instead of travelling to people, we did our socializing and visiting with people in our block of flats and with near neighbours.

We were not especially lonely. There was a constant stream of neighbours, relatives and friends of Afaf who visited our flat. In fact, the stresses of the war bonded us together so that some good came out of the war's evil. One example of this was a young woman called, like my daughter, Ibtisam. This Ibtisam lived in the flat below us; she had married when she was quite young and had had four young children in quick succession. Her husband, who was much older, was hardly ever at home to give her a hand with anything and she simply couldn't cope with her young family and a war. The children were so neglected and constantly crying that I started to visit her in order to help. There was always plenty to do: the children needed washing, dressing and feeding. I would often cook a meal for them as well. I persevered, believing that with care, love and support this young woman could recover sufficiently to care for her own family. It was a hard task requiring patience and much prayer. Eventually, Ibtisam's husband divorced her, but she came to have a real faith in Jesus. Many years later, she wrote to me from the United States where she had found a new caring husband and a home and, in her letters, she witnessed to the Lord's grace and mercy in her life and to her love for Him. Her eldest daughter, Fatmeh, also kept in contact and later wrote to me from Frankfurt in Germany where she was living with her husband and two young children. In her letters, she addressed me as 'Grandmother' and expressed her gratitude to me for standing by her mother and the family at that time.

The war eased slightly in 1976 but we all knew it wasn't over. Every night, we could hear the shelling or shooting along the Green Line. Frequently and often without any warning, the fighting would flare up. There were many different militia groups: some effectively small armies, others little more than gangs with machineguns. As in 1958, outsiders meddled in Lebanon's tragedy, shipping in weapons and organising battles. The forces that drove the conflict became ever more complex; the rich fought the poor, the Muslims fought the Christians, the Palestinians fought the Lebanese or Syrians and the leftists fought the rightists. Loose coalitions of militias would form and then, often within days, fall apart and fight each other. No one, not even the combatants, really knew what exactly was going on.

Increasingly, though, Arafat's PLO came to impose some kind of crude and often brutal stability on West Beirut. The result was that, for much of the time, it was possible to live a more or less normal life. Gunmen walked the streets but at least within West Beirut a sort of tense calm prevailed. One result of this PLO control, about which I had very mixed feelings, was that being able to speak with a Palestinian accent became a real advantage. Fearful lest they offend someone who could have the power to have them arrested and beaten – or worse, people treated anyone with a Palestinian accent with an almost fearful respect.

From 1976, the Lebanon Intervarsity Fellowship (LIVF) restarted under the leadership of the Reverend Colin Chapman working among students in West Beirut and Afaf began to work for them. There were tremendous opportunities for Christian work among students; although evening meetings were too risky, daytime social activities and communal meals encouraged many to get together and hear

God's word. I found myself drawn in too helping with the food, preparing and cooking the meals.

During those days, I would often worry about Afaf at work. When things were bad – when it was what we called a 'hot' day – I would find myself pacing up and down the balcony until I saw Afaf come home. She used to tell me off for my concern but they were indeed very dangerous times.

One of the few leisure activities in those difficult days was simply to go out for drives and try to get out of the city. One Sunday afternoon, Afaf and some of her friends planned to go for a drive to the mountains with two cars. At the last minute, one of the girls had to drop out and I asked my daughter if I could take her place. As I said it, I realised that it actually sounded more like 'I'm coming up with you whether you like it or not!' The reality was that I was desperate to get out of the house. They found a place for me and we drove out into the countryside and, in the warm sunshine and fresh air, began to unwind and put the war behind us. Yet on the way back home, the grim realities of the war emerged. One of the girls decided to take a short cut back and we ended up down a rather lonely road. Suddenly, out of nowhere, a group of armed men from one of the Muslim militias appeared before us and waved us down. The men asked the usual questions, who we were, where we were going and so on. Realising that we were unfamiliar with the area, they offered to show us the way. They suggested that they should travel in one car with one of the girls driving while the rest of us followed in the other car. The idea that one of the girls would be alone in a car full of armed men was alarming. As the eldest person in our group, I spoke out and objected to their plan, using my strongest Palestinian accent. There were no further suggestions and they led us safely toward our road. I thanked God for his mercy.

Despite our faith, the strain and pressure on both my life and Afaf's soon built up to high levels. During a renewed spell of fighting in Beirut both my brother Nakhleh and his family as well as cousin Munir, his wife and son came to stay with us. They had been living in the Christian section of the city but had found it too risky. The Phalangists distrusted all Palestinians and often stopped them on the streets, in their cars or on buses and rounded them up for questioning. Some were beaten, others shot and killed, others just disappeared.

A further stress on me at that time came with the news that Halim, the brother I was closest to, had been diagnosed with cancer of the lymph glands. His family tried every treatment available whatever it cost and he went to the United States to see some of the world's most prominent consultants in cancer treatment but all to no avail. Eventually, he and his wife returned to Beirut. I cannot put into words my feelings or my prayers for my brother. I begged God to take me instead of him, if it would give him his life back. The answer God gave me was plain and unarguable: he had already done just that for Halim through Jesus. I understood and my prayers changed: all I wanted now was for Halim to come to know Jesus as his saviour.

Time though was not on my side: Halim was in hospital and deteriorating fast. I visited him a few times but I soon realised that those final days were for his wife and family. It was hard to let go. Fortunately, a family occasion came to my assistance. Ibtisam and Scott were now living in France and my daughter was now pregnant with her fifth baby. She and Scott asked me if I could come over and help with the family while she was in hospital. I was more than delighted to do so and there in France, the heaviness in my heart was lifted as I became involved with my grandchildren. In September 1979, baby Andrew was born and my joy over his birth was a compensation when the news of Halim's death reached me.

With renewed fighting, Afaf left Beirut and spent three months in England in a short-term job in London in the city. When things quietened down, she returned to Beirut.

By early 1980s, normal life as we knew it had become a

memory. The war continued, as wearying and deadly as ever. The sound of shellfire and shootings were a daily occurrence but the weapons now were bigger and more widespread: even children were armed. There were now long periods when there was no water and no power or telephone. By now, many people were reconciled to the fact that things were not getting better and could easily get much worse. There were rumours of another Israeli invasion of southern Lebanon to attack the Palestinian camps there, an action that could easily spill over into Beirut. Israeli planes flew over Beirut every day, breaking the sound barrier with loud explosions, sometimes practising attacks and sometimes bombing the camps a few miles away from us.

Two incidents finally brought home to us the utter hopelessness of the situation. Bullets were fired into the flat and embedded themselves in a wall: where they were fired from, or why, I never found out. The second incident was seeing the headless body of a man being pulled behind a car past our house. For Afaf, that was the final straw and from then on, she began to make every effort to leave.

There was certainly family pressure for me to leave as well. Siham and Ron were particularly insistent that I get out and come and live with them. Yet I hesitated, I was now in my seventies and had no desire to move again: I didn't want to leave my home, and I felt that I couldn't start all over again. Afaf was offered a job by her previous employers at their London office. She accepted and, in early 1982, left. Before leaving Afaf filled in an application form issued by the British Consulate for me for a visa that would allow me to go and live in Britain with my daughter and her husband.

Now on my own, I began to feel forsaken and helpless and, for a brief period, I experienced blackouts and complete disorientation. At one point, I went out into the street looking for Afaf and asking the neighbours if anyone had seen her. My nephew Mazen was very concerned about me and consulted Dr. Abu Shanab across the street from us about my situation; he prescribed me some medication that calmed me down. Mazen took me to Adib's house where I stayed for a few days until I recovered and then returned home.

Yet Mazen too was leaving. His wife and two children had gone ahead of him and he was simply winding up his affairs before following them. Our building was almost empty; most of the people I knew had already left. I realised that this was no place for a seventy-four year old woman to be left alone. Finally, I agreed that if Siham and Ron could arrange it, I would go and live with them in England.

CHAPTER 19

Moving on

Siham and Ron started working to get me a residential visa for the UK. The rector of their church in Bedford, the Reverend Donald Strong, referred them to their MP, Trevor Skeet. Mr Skeet was helpful, even inviting Ron to his office at the Houses of Parliament. His advice was that Ron had to write to the Immigration Department of the Home Office with our particular request, proving as best we could that I physically, socially and financially was dependent on them.

Six months passed before the Immigration Office responded with letters to them and to me in Beirut. My residential visa was refused: they were not satisfied that I was 'wholly or mainly dependent' upon Siham and Ron. For Siham and Ron it was devastating news as they had become increasingly concerned for my health. That evening they shared the news at a church prayer meeting. There, after prayer it was decided that an appeal against the ruling should be launched.

In early 1982, Mazen came up to the flat one afternoon to see me. He was worried because I was still very weak and because I seemed to have lost interest in everything around me, even my food. He wanted me out of Beirut before he left. He suggested that, having been refused entry to Britain, I ought to go to France to stay with Ibtisam and Scott and their family. I was in no state to question, argue or make decisions for myself. I accepted his decision with tears. I knew I was losing a precious earthly home that God had allowed me to have for many years. Mazen was loving and very efficient and very soon an entry visa to France was stamped in my passport and arrangements were being made for me to leave.

Suddenly it was time to go. Mazen and my sister's son-in-law Rohy helped me into the comfortable Mercedes car and loaded my luggage. We were driven to the airport by the caretaker, Hussein, who assured me that nothing would happen to my flat and that all my belongings would be safe. Having seen Hussein in his capacity as our street guard with his Kalashnikov slung over his shoulder I believed him. Together they saw me onto the plane.

At the time, none of us knew how fortunate I was to leave when I did. Shortly after I left, on the 6th June 1982, the Israelis invaded Lebanon with massive land and air forces and, within a few days, were laying siege to West Beirut. Throughout the summer, West Beirut was sealed off and the airport closed while round the clock air attacks and artillery bombardment tried to destroy the PLO. The death toll was appalling and had I not left when I did, it is doubtful whether I would have survived.

Scott and Ibtisam met me at Lyons airport and drove me to their home at St. Ismier, just outside Grenoble. They had prepared the spare bedroom downstairs for me, a comfortable room with easy access to the garden. They told me later that they had been worried by how frail and thin I had been and the fact that I seemed to be distracted. Yet over the next few days as I rested and ate properly, I began to get my strength back. Slowly but steadily, I started going out with the family for walks, enjoying the fresh air and the countryside and being with the children. I would take the youngest in his pushchair down to the vineyards and walnut groves. It was as if I had gone to sleep and suddenly woken up in a different world. Although Scott and Ibtisam would have loved to keep me, it was agreed that France was not the right place for me. Not knowing French I would have been totally isolated and confined to our house. The idea that I would have had no Christian fellowship apart from my family and could not talk to people about Jesus was not a happy one. But would I be able to go to Britain?

In England, Siham and Ron had appealed against the Home Office ruling, filled in the application forms again and had their MP add a personal letter of recommendation. Their house group continued to pray over the matter and their prayers were an encouragement and reassurance. On July 3rd 1982, they received a letter from the Home Office authorising the granting of a residence visa. I learned later that Siham and Ron's house group were actually praying for me when Ron came in with the letter in his hand. God had already answered their prayers! Within days, Scott and Ibtisam had arranged for me to travel to London.

I settled quickly in Bedford with Ron, Siham and their three children. The house was conveniently situated near the town centre so I could walk there and do my own shopping. I found the churches a problem. Ron and Siham and their family were members of a local Church of England church, St. John's. I was determined not to go there as I had a deep aversion to all Anglican churches. My attitude was partly a result of being a long-term member of an open Brethren group and also because of preconception and even prejudices about many aspects of English life that arose from my experiences in childhood and youth all those years ago in Palestine.

One day, on the way to town, I noticed a large non-conformist church and made up my mind to go there the following Sunday and see what it was like. My first few visits were very enjoyable; there were people to welcome newcomers at the door and I was led to a seat near the front where I could see and hear clearly. I began to feel at home. But not totally; I felt there was something lacking. Perhaps, I thought, I needed to be part of my family at worship. Yet to do that would mean accompanying them to their Anglican church and that was something that I was reluctant to do. A real battle was going through my heart; the old obstinate, headstrong Wadeah was still alive and well! The matter resolved itself one Sunday, at Harvest Service. Unaware of the special day, I went to church as usual only to find that the church was so full that there were only a few seats available near the door. But it was cold and every time the door opened, I felt an icy draught. During the second hymn I left; it wasn't just the cold, my pride was hurt: no one had paid any attention to me.

So I walked home and, in my room, I turned on the radio. It was the BBC Sunday Service and John Stott was preaching from an Anglican Church! I had no idea who the preacher was, but all I knew was that he brought God's word to me in a new and powerful way. There was peace in my heart at last. The following Sunday I accompanied Ron, Siham, and the children to St. John's with joy in my heart: I had submitted to God's will over where he wanted me to be.

From that time on, that church became my home: I prayed daily for the ministers and the congregation there and that God would pour out his blessings through the Holy Spirit on them. I have worshipped there for sixteen years, during the leadership of four different Rectors and various curates and have learnt many valuable lessons and my Christian life continued to grow.

It was a great joy, too, to discover how many committed true Christians there were within the church. I was also delighted to find the variety of Christian activities that there were. One particular midweek daytime meeting that I supported was organised by 'Christian Viewpoint' as an evangelistic outreach to draw non-working and non-church going women to Christ. It was a monthly meeting but Christians were also encouraged to attend the prayer meetings in the intervening weeks. Sometimes with my daughter or sometimes alone, I went to these meetings and the loving fellowship shown to me there was a foretaste of heaven that God had reserved for my old age. Some years later when the family that had hosted these meetings emigrated to the United States, our house became the new venue for these gatherings. The Lord put on my shoulders the responsibility of supporting this work in prayer.

CHAPTER 20

Sunset

By the summer of 1983 Afaf was happily employed working in London for the Arab Investment Company, the firm that had employed her in Beirut and which now had a new branch open in London. Yet she had set her heart on coming to live in Bedford and commuting, like so many, to London. This coincided with Ron and Siham looking for a change of house; they wanted a place where I could have a small self-contained apartment.

When a house on The Embankment in Bedford came on the market, I was taken to see it and asked to give my opinion. The second floor was already partitioned off from the main house as a separate flat and when Ron asked me what I thought about the house, I could not hold the words back: 'It's the Lord's house for you, you should take it.' After seeing the house Afaf too, agreed and was happy to go ahead with the purchase. I was to live with Ron and Siham as part of the family. In August, we moved to the new house.

With the river flowing by just across the road and the well-kept municipal gardens visible from the front of the house, I found my new home almost paradise. I could never have dreamed that such a place would be my home in my old age and I have no words to describe my gratitude to God for this wonderful home. The large back garden with its lawn, flowerbeds and fruit trees have been a daily reminder of God's undeserved mercy, love and never ending blessings. As the first trees burst into blossoms of pink and white flowers every spring, as the birds woke me up in the mornings with cascading delightful songs and conversational tunes I, too, lifted up my heart and blended my silent (and sometimes not so silent) heartfelt praise with theirs to God my saviour. All the struggles and difficulties of the past seemed to go, leaving no bitterness or ugly scars in my life. I sensed my Shepherd's strong arms helping me along the remaining paths of life.

The years raced by and in my old age, England became truly my home and my beloved adopted country. In 1989, the government introduced the Community Tax and like everyone else, I had to pay my monthly dues. I did not always have enough money to cover the bill but my family made up the deficit. Siham thought it unfair that, when I had no source of income whatsoever, I should have to pay the full community tax. So she wrote to the appropriate department in the council and put the situation before them. She also mentioned, almost in passing, that many years ago in Palestine, I had worked as a nurse in British government hospitals where I paid taxes on my income and that, by rights, I should have been entitled to some pension at my age.

Soon a letter informed me that a social security officer would pay me a visit shortly. The officer, a smart and well-spoken lady, filled in some forms for me while I answered her questions. The interview was soon over without the Community Tax being mentioned once. When I asked her about it, she said that there would be no community tax charge for me and then, with a smile and a nod of her head, she was gone. The following week I received a letter from the Social Security explaining how they arrived at the figure of a weekly income that I was to receive from them. My eyes saw the words and figures through my tears but my mind would not take it in. We were all left amazed at the fairness of the British Government and the miraculous working of our Heavenly Father.

I had always worked hard to earn an income to look after my family but as I grew older, there was no prospect of any private means or earnings I could call my own. It did not unduly trouble me. I knew I had the love and support of my children and various members of my family. God too had never let me down. But this new miracle was too much for me, beyond my comprehension. I was overwhelmed with his love that melted my heart. I felt that God had honoured me and lifted up my face.

God had given me a new lease of life here in Bedford. All I wanted now was to use every minute of my remaining years to reach the hearts of others with the news of God's love. I had a particular burden for the surviving members of my family, my two brothers and my sister. I made every effort to visit them in Israel and Beirut. My new British passport facilitated my long distance travelling. To me that was a great blessing.

God gave me strength and courage to make these long journeys and he opened for me many opportunities to talk about him and about the love of our Saviour. In Israel, I met with my brother Emile. He had been antagonistic to Christianity in the past but now he had become much more open, willing to listen and ready to discuss Biblical matters without opposition. Although he did not admit it, I suspected that he had been reading the Bible too and I am confident that the Lord softened his heart. Emile died in 1996, a well-known and respected writer.

There were many happy family occasions. I attended the wedding of Thea my first grandchild and the first to get married. I thanked God for allowing me to be there. In 1997, I became a great-grandmother to Pauline, one of Ibtisam's granddaughters, and to Alexandria, one of Huda's granddaughters.

Yet there were also times of sorrow. In September 1995, my dear son-in-law Ron passed away. In many ways, Ron was the grown up son I never had and his death made me broken hearted. Yet I found the privilege of being there to support and comfort Siham an honour too, albeit a heavy and painful one.

Many friends and family members from overseas visited me in Bedford. Being so close to London many people travelling to the States came to visit me en route. At every visit and meeting, I feel that God has enabled me to witness to his love and salvation. Some listened to me out of respect for my age, some out of genuine interest. Sometimes on fine days in the summer months, I would cross the road in front of our house and sit on a bench along the embankment by the river. I would often talk to whoever happened to be sitting there of the love of Christ and our need for his salvation. Those who turned out to be Christians rejoiced with me while those who weren't listened patiently to this strange old lady who told them about Christ. Some were English, Italians, Indians and Arabs, others I could not tell their country of origin and they chose not to say.

On December 1st 1998, my sister Nada stopped in Bedford on her way to Canada where one of her married daughters lived. She stayed with me for two weeks. As always, it gladdened my heart to see her, but this time I felt a deep sorrow within my heart. Finally, at the end of the fortnight, as we stood together in front of the house on the morning of her departure, I realised that this was the last time that I would kiss her goodbye. We hugged and kissed again, tears streaming down both our faces and then she was gone.

On December 15th 1998, I celebrated, with great gratitude to God, my ninety-first birthday.

There was talk and preparation for my grandson, Andrew's wedding in April to Niamh-Ann in Ireland, her home. Siham started planning for our travelling and accommodation but I quickly stopped her and said that I would not be going with them to the wedding. Normally, Siham would argue and try to convince me to change my mind but this time she didn't. She accepted the decision: I was sure that I wouldn't be going to the wedding.

I know my days on earth are now limited. Yet I know where I am going. I have not kept my longing to go home to my Lord a secret; my friends at the house group meeting have heard me more than once saying that I'm ready to go.

I am apprehensive but I am ready.

Epilogue
by
Siham Brown

On the eve of December 23rd 1998, Mother was suddenly taken ill with nausea and high temperature. As I entered her room, I noticed her hand resting on the side of her abdomen. 'I think I've got a strangulated hernia,' she said. Her face was flushed deep red yet she was shivering all over. I was instantly on the phone to our GP, but since it was after surgery hours, I was connected to the duty emergency service. I told the doctor what the symptoms were and also mentioned the word 'hernia'.

'I'll be with you right away,' he said and was in mother's room in less than ten minutes. He quickly confirmed mother's diagnosis. Rather than wait for an ambulance, I drove mother to the hospital myself with a hastily written note from the doctor. She was quickly admitted into the Emergency Ward and prepared for surgery.

The doctor who examined her explained that the operation might be a simple or a more complex one depending on the extent of the internal inflammation. Later that evening, the ward sister phoned us to say surgery was over and that mother was back on the ward and comfortable. By Christmas Day, she seemed to be progressing well.

At 4 am on Boxing Day, the hospital phoned. The ward sister informed me that Mother had a severe stroke but we could come and see her as soon as we wished. There was no real improvement over the next four days and the family gathered around her. We shared the visiting so that someone stayed by Mother's side the whole time. That evening Mother was moved to a side ward and, as we stood round her bed, we sang two of her favourite choruses; ones we had learned as children. “Constantly abiding, Jesus is mine” and “Trust and obey, for there’s no other way to be happy in Jesus, but to trust and obey”.

Her face was relaxed and at peace. We kissed her goodnight and left.

The final summons from the hospital came at 5 am on Tuesday 31st December. Mother had passed away sometime between 3 and 4 am.

We gathered around her bed again a final time; only this time it was as if we were in the presence of a queen, beautiful and ready to meet her King.